THE SOCIAL BADGE

The Social Badger

——

Ecology and Behaviour of a Group-living Carnivore
(*Meles meles*)

——

HANS KRUUK

Institute of Terrestrial Ecology
Banchory, Kincardineshire

Oxford   New York   Tokyo
OXFORD UNIVERSITY PRESS
1989

Oxford University Press, Walton Street, Oxford OX2 6DP
Oxford New York Toronto
Delhi Bombay Calcutta Madras Karachi
Petaling Jaya Singapore Hong Kong Tokyo
Nairobi Dar es Salaam Cape Town
Melbourne Auckland
and associated companies in
Berlin Ibadan

Oxford is a trade mark of Oxford University Press

Published in the United States
by Oxford University Press, New York

British Library Cataloguing in Publication Data
Kruuk, Hans
The social badger.
1. Great Britain. Badgers. Behaviour
I. Title
599.74′447
ISBN 0–19–858703–1

Library of Congress Cataloging in Publication Data
Kruuk, H. (Hans)
The social badger: ecology and behaviour of a group-living
carnivore (Meles meles) | Hans Kruuk.
p.   cm. Bibliography: p.
Includes index.
1. Old World badger.   I. Title.
QL737.C25K79   1988   599.74′447—dc20   89–31630
ISBN 0–19–858703–1

Typeset by
Cotswold Typesetting Limited, Gloucester
Printed in Great Britain by
Butler and Tanner Limited, Frome, Somerset

To the memory of
NIKO TINBERGEN

PREFACE

BADGERS (*Meles meles*) have fascinated me since my early days in Holland, and, more than any other wild mammal, they are of absorbing interest to naturalists in Britain and other countries. Several admirable books have been written about badgers, notably by Ernest Neal and others. My excuse for this small addition to the collection is that my aim is different from that of previous writers; this is not a general 'Natural History of The Badger', nor is it an account of my personal experience with the animals, much as I enjoy talking about that. I have set out to write about particular questions concerning badgers and about 10 years of field research trying to answer them.

The problems concern the badgers' peculiar social life and how it relates to their ecology. The research was a step-by-step process, and I obtained a tremendous amount of satisfaction from it: posing relevant questions, outwitting the animal in its own habitat at night, inventing ways of trapping, following and experimenting, building up relationships with captives. Here I have tried to explain why the problems are relevant, how I set about answering them, and I hope that I have presented the results in such a way that they make sense to anyone with a cultivated interest in natural history.

The social badger is aimed at naturalists as well as specialists and I hope it will provide some ideas and inspiration for observation and research by others. I wrote it for several reasons. I wanted to make our previous publications on the subject, in scientific journals, more accessible to anyone interested in badgers, but also there were quite a few results which had not yet been published. Most importantly, however, I wanted to present all the results as one complete picture and to point out some practical applications.

This book is about our research, mostly in Scotland, partly in Oxford, and I have not attempted to review the many scientific publications by others on related topics. As a compromise between a fully referenced review and a simple readable account I have mentioned at the end of each chapter those scientific papers from our own research group which are pertinent and in which further references can be found. Also, I have added a few references to other books and papers which are important in the context of that chapter; undoubtedly, however, I have omitted many excellent studies, for which I apologize.

Too many people have been involved in these badger studies to make it possible for me to acknowledge them all; I hope that they realize how grateful I am for their various contributions. But I would like to make some exceptions, most of all for the late Niko Tinbergen, FRS, Professor at Oxford, mentor, and friend, to the memory of whom I have dedicated this book. He taught me the kind of behavioural ecology to which I am now addicted, he made the early badger studies in Wytham possible, and he contributed part of his Nobel prize award to the purchase of essential equipment. My wife Jane has helped in all manners and at all stages; without her, this book would not have been. Other important, industrious, and cheerful colleagues in this venture were Tim Parish, Peter Mallinson, the late Charlie Griffin, and Alan Leitch and Chris Brown, to all of whom I convey my gratitude. Finally, I thank Robin Tanner for contributing several excellent photographs.

Banchory   H.K.
November 1988

CONTENTS

PLATES

Plates fall between pp. 84 *and* 85

I

Introduction

In the studies described in this book I have been concerned with badgers' behaviour, with their food and the way in which they obtain it, with their social organization, and even with scent marking and the reasons for their strangely patterned faces. On the face of it this may seem an odd assortment of interests, combined perhaps in another of those general natural history studies. But there is more order in these enquiries than may appear at first. My ultimate aim is the understanding of social organization and an insight into the reasons why badgers should live in groups. I believe that all the different topics mentioned above are highly relevant in that context, as I hope to show. In particular, the badgers' food and the peculiar patterns of its availability are important factors in deciding the way in which badgers organize themselves, and much of what is said here concerns that relation between food and their social system.

The European badger (*Meles meles*) is a fascinating animal for a study of these kinds of problems, because, although it is a social carnivore, it appears to be very different from the many others that have evolved a gregarious social organization. The social system of badgers is more primitive, perhaps, than that of wolves, lions, spotted hyaenas, or dwarf mongooses. For that reason alone badgers are worthy of further study, apart from all the other aspects of their life which have intrigued generations of naturalists, especially in Britain.

In the following chapters I will describe how some initial studies near Oxford, in England, led to research on badgers in Scotland; these first pilot studies taught me what questions to ask and how to set about answering them. Furthermore, in field studies with mammals it is almost inevitable that much time is spent on devising methods of study: with birds a great deal can often be done with just binoculars and a notebook, but with mammals, especially nocturnal ones, it is much more difficult, and methodology becomes one of the major challenges of working with these animals. After explaining why I started the studies in Scotland I set out in detail what the objectives were and which methods were used to achieve them: how I caught badgers, followed them at night, and estimated their numbers and their food. I then describe the diet of badgers in different areas, and their feeding behaviour, before analysing the way in which they are organized in their communal territories. In the final chapters I describe the relationships between badgers, within and between their communal territories, and the way they communicate in the wild and in captivity. Finally, I draw all this together to suggest why and how badgers have evolved into their peculiar social pattern of 'clans' and how some of our results could be used for conservation or management of this species.

The word 'clan' may conjure up images of swaying kilts and swirling pipes, but it has long been taken from its Gaelic origins and used elsewhere for groupings of people and animals. I use the word in preference to the term 'social group' which is often used by other students of badger behaviour; the meaning of the word 'group' is so general that it does not convey much, and the adjective 'social' does not help, because it is not possible to conceive of any asocial grouping. The clan concept is a very useful one to denote a number of individuals collectively inhabiting and usually defending an area. The individuals are mostly related (though a few immigrants are accepted), but they do not necessarily go round together in a gang, a pack, or a herd. As another example, the hyaenas I studied in Africa lived in clans, and anthropologists often use the term to describe units of related individuals smaller than tribes, but larger than families. Badger clans are not confined to Scotland and the species does live in clans throughout its Eurasian range—but it seemed particularly apt to describe them here, in the Scottish Highlands, as clannish.

The objectives of this study were never far from my mind when watching badgers. Perhaps that rather blinkered me and caused me to overlook things that were happening in front of my eyes; at the same time it was necessary to approach the animals with particular questions. One of the main skills in scientific fieldwork lies in sifting observations: what is important for a particular purpose and what is not. There is a world of difference between watching animals simply for some aesthetic pleasure (or to satisfy some basic hunting instinct) and studying them and asking specific questions. One difference is in the anticipation it involves: when just watching for pleasure every observation is accepted as it occurs, but when scientific questions are posed, there are already some possible answers in mind and what the animal will do if any of these ideas are correct is predicted. The quarry is hunted in a different manner and, for me, the excitement of then watching it at close quarters is even greater. Watching a badger whilst it is providing the answers to my ideas, and whilst its behaviour is increasing the store of hard data, adds an extra dimension to the experience.

I will give an example of the kind of observation from which this study has been built up, that is an account of a session at a badger sett indicating the variety of relevant information which can be collected during just one evening, as well as some of the immediate satisfaction derived from watching the animals in the surroundings of the Highlands.

It was June 1983, eight years after I had started my study in Scotland. From a bluff I looked over a huge sweep of scenery, in which the River Spey brushed its way north through a wild landscape of birch trees and alders, a country of salmon, otter, and eagle. The badger sett between the birches below me did not really stand out—it just merged into its background; but in my mind it had become the focal point, centre stage. And it did, indeed, appear like a stage, albeit somewhat chaotic, with a dozen tunnel entrances and large, bare, spoil heaps. It was the headquarters of the Loch clan, with seven badgers asleep in its underground chambers. As I had done on many previous evenings, I was waiting for darkness to fall, waiting to see what was stirring between the bracken fronds, whilst being distracted by midges and the sounds of foxes and roe-deer.

My visit to the Loch clan that evening was a formal routine visit; but with this kind of study nothing was ever completely routine. I needed to know how many cubs there were in each sett, and the only way to find out was to sit and wait, to let the young ones come and play, and hope that I would see them all at the same time. Eleven o'clock, and still no real darkness; but then there was movement below me, distinct shadows were joined by greyer shapes and there were glimpses of black-and-white stripes. Smallish and furry meant they were cubs; larger and more staid would be adult badgers trundling back and forth. Two cubs romping near a patch of bracken—I wondered if I saw a third, then concluded that there was an adult with them. Not surprising, really; at no time that year had I seen more than two

Fig. 1.1. Badger cubs, approximately four months old, near the sett entrance, grooming each other. (Photograph by R. Tanner.)

FIG. 1.2. Two cubs play-fighting next to a sett entrance, with adults in background. (Photograph by R. Tanner.)

cubs at that sett. In my mind I added another point to a graph, one which compared the number of cubs to the number of adults in the clan. Curiously, in all our clans there were usually no more than two cubs, however many boars and sows might populate the huge setts, an observation which I thought was very important. From the outset I had been worried about this: what was the point of living in these clans if badgers could do no better than produce this number of offspring?

My meditations were interrupted by the arrival of a badger from elsewhere. I could not see whether it was a male or a female, but clearly the animal was known to the assembled badgers emerging from the tunnels; without knowing its identity, I could only speculate that it must be a clan member which had been sleeping somewhere else, in an outlying hole. No noise at all, just a deathly silence enveloped the animals—I could see five adults now. The newcomer sniffed another badger intensively along its flank; then both turned around and backed up against each other, tails up. This was a behaviour which I had called a 'mutual squat-mark', some form of greeting which badgers use after they have not met each other for at least several days. Softly I muttered the data into my dictaphone, noticing at the same time that one of the adults and the cubs walked off together. I could not be certain which adult badger was with the cubs, but in all previous observations it had been the mother, and no other badger ever appeared to take care of the young.

Slowly I walked home from my observation post, following a narrow path in the

FIG. 1.3. Part of a clan, adults and cubs, near the sett before leaving on their nocturnal foraging trips. (Photograph by R. Tanner.)

misty midsummer grey of the combined dusk and dawn, well into the next day, heading for the bothy. I saw that I was following a badger path which led me past a badger latrine; I noticed that I looked at a pasture through the eyes of a badger, judging it for its earthworm potential. There was a heavy dew that night, and I knew that the animals I had just watched would be feeding there soon and the next day I would find fresh droppings in the latrine.

All the things that I saw that night—the gambolling cubs, the curious greeting behaviour of the two adults, one adult going off with the cubs, the latrine near the pasture—were on the face of it quite unrelated. At least they might appear so, but to me, even when I was peering at the shadows moving below my rock, they were like pieces of a giant jigsaw puzzle, pieces from different parts of the picture, and I could put them together. I was studying the adaptation of a whole complex of behaviour patterns to what the environment had to offer, and it was impossible to ask my question about the sociality of badgers without taking detailed behaviour and social mechanisms into account. Furthermore, if the behaviour of the animals is indeed adapted to environmental needs, then the badgers' relationship with their environment, especially their feeding ecology, has to be the basis for an analysis of the social system, which increases the complexity of the study even further.

In the following chapters I will discuss how different aspects of the ecology and the social life of the badger in Scotland are related to each other. I begin, however, with the pilot studies further south, in Wytham Woods near Oxford, England.

Further details

See Kruuk (1986, 1987). See also Neal (1986); Paget and Middleton (1974).

2

The badgers of Wytham

In the early 1970s I returned to Oxford from East Africa, where I had spent seven years studying hyaenas and various other carnivores in the Serengeti. Another of my aims in Africa had been to understand why some animals live in societies in which individuals co-operate, whereas other species do not. With the African carnivores it had seemed simple and I felt that I knew the answers: I had come to the conclusion that those that were gregarious, the ones that lived in groups, did so because they could help each other to hunt. Spotted hyaenas, hunting dogs, lions—all these species have intricate communities of many members, hunting together, fighting together, able to overcome huge adversaries, in contrast to related species which were solitary. I thought I had convincing evidence that the exploitation of large prey through co-operation was the main biological function of their sociality and that of many other species. Then, back in Britain, I looked for the first time at a society of badgers and my carefully constructed hypothesis collapsed like a house of cards.

The University of Oxford owns a large area of woods and farmland capping two hills just outside the edge of the city—Wytham Woods. In my new job in the Zoology Department I had easy access there and spent a great deal of time walking the woods, copses, and farmland of the large Wytham estate. Huge badger sets with 20 entrances or more dotted the slopes and several of these setts could be readily watched in the evening. Badgers came trundling out, singly, to disappear in the gloom; what immediately struck me was the fact that there were so many of them within one sett. Of course, this was known to more experienced naturalists (for instance, Neal 1948), but perhaps it struck me especially because of my previous experiences with the African social carnivores. Here was another, clearly gregarious species, and if badgers would help each other to hunt they could have roamed the countryside in packs, pulling down deer and sheep. Instead, the dung-pits next to their holes told a different story: it seemed that beetles and wheat were their daily fare. These very intriguing observations were only the beginning; I had expected something else from these badgers, but they did not fit in with that.

The little that had been published about badgers at that time was not of much help with my problem. Most of it was anecdotal and, apart from some excellent studies of badger food, and those on reproductive physiology by Neal and Harrison (1958), there was nothing on their social behaviour, their organization, the way in which they move through the countryside. Neal wrote that badgers were non-territorial, with animals from neighbouring setts going on friendly visits to each other. I had also seen evidence of such visits, but the explanation still sounded rather unlikely, and there were no good, hard data.

Wytham Woods is a beautiful and to my mind 'typical' piece of English countryside (Plate 3). Its area is over 1000 hectares, of which about one-third is deciduous woodland. It has been called the best-studied wood in the world, because of the lifelong attentions of such famous ecologists as Charles Elton, David Lack, Mick Southern, George Varley, and their scores of students and colleagues. The woods are spread over and around the hills, with oak, sycamore, ash, beech, and a dense understorey of hazel, brambles, and various other trees and shrubs. In spring parts of Wytham Woods are covered in oceans of bluebells. Everywhere there are rough tracks and footpaths and, more to the point, everywhere there are also badger paths tunnelling through the undergrowth.

Along the slopes there is a fairly narrow band of sandy soil at the surface, a band which girdles the two hills. Above it there is much hard rock, with fossil corals; below it, thick clay. One of the first things I noticed when I traversed the woods in search of badgers was that almost all badger setts were in that girdle of grit–sand, presumably because it was well drained and easy to dig compared with the surrounding area. Much more important, these setts were not just made anywhere in the sandy belt: when I mapped them, the large, most important setts were rather regularly spaced (Fig. 2.1). If the distances between the setts were examined and it was calculated what these distances would have been if the badgers had distributed themselves randomly along the sandy belt, it was clear that they kept themselves apart from each other (Fig. 2.2). That suggested territoriality to me: surely these animals were not just good friends if they spaced themselves so carefully? The question was how to set about studying it.

Thinking back over those years, it is astonishing how much progress has been made in our techniques of observing and following animals in the field. Then, radio-tracking was virtually unknown in Britain, electronic night-watching equipment was something used by the military, and 'beta-lights' were used on aeroplanes; all these techniques were unheard of amongst naturalists. In Africa I had done some radio-tracking, using equipment from the United States, so I was not entirely unprepared—but there I had been able to do almost all my night-work on the open savannahs using moonlight. The moon rarely seems to shine as strongly on Britain as it does on the Serengeti, so it is not much help when watching badgers in a wood.

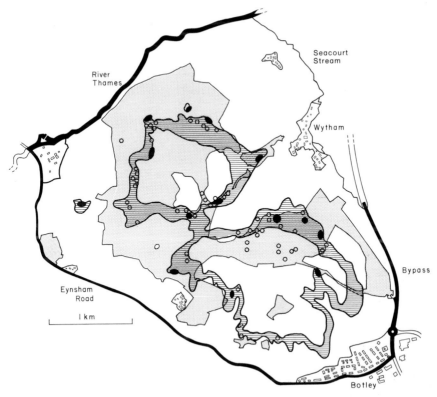

FIG. 2.1. Map of Wytham Woods, near Oxford (1975). Grey areas are woodlands, the hatched area is a belt of grit–sand around the two hills. Badger main setts are black and outliers are open circles, showing the spacing between the main setts (from Kruuk 1978*a*).

I was fortunate to have the help of Peter Mallinson, my friend and assistant, and together we tried to overcome our practical difficulties. Technicians in the Zoology Department had to develop radio-transmitters from scratch; there were many failures, interspersed with the occasional success. Somehow we got some transmitters going and managed to sort out how to catch badgers in stopped snares and how to immobilize them without harming either them or ourselves (by pinning them down at the end of the snare, straddling the animals without getting bitten, and putting a tin containing ether on cotton wool over their snouts—all usually in the pitch dark; see Fig. 2.3). We had endless problems getting the radio-transmitter to stay on: collars came off and the badgers hated harnesses. We finally designed a harness that worked, more or less (Fig. 2.4), but it was far from ideal. One neat, little finishing touch to this harness was the small

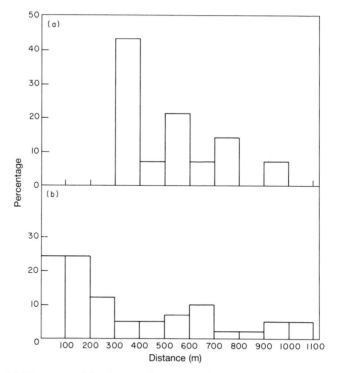

Fig. 2.2. (a) Histogram of the distances between main setts in Wytham Woods, showing that all setts are at least 300 m apart. (b) Histogram showing what the distances between main setts would have been if the badgers had made them randomly in the woods in the belt of grit–sand. Actual badger setts are clearly more spaced out (from Kruuk 1978a).

'beta-light', a small glass disk of about 2.5 cm diameter and which we could buy commercially. It emitted a greenish light from an ionized gas inside, and we attached it to the transmitter on top of the harness above the shoulder. The light looked like that from a fairly large glow-worm and was of tremendous help when following the badger in the dark, without disturbing the animal itself or any other animals it met—for us it was often the only thing we saw of the badger. On several occasions unsuspecting citizens living at the edge of the wood had problems in explaining their observations of a green spot moving in the dark!

Our major breakthrough in observing badgers came from a most unexpected quarter. Night-watching equipment was being used in security operations by the police, consisting of an infrared 'invisible' searchlight and an electronic converter and intensifier to make the image visible to the human eye. The whole instrument was similar to a large pair of binoculars with a spotlight on top, using 'black light'. It was extremely efficient, even on the darkest of nights, but its major snag was its price. I desperately

Fig. 2.3. Peter Mallinson restrains a badger caught in a stopped snare by pinning the snare wire down to the ground. Note the Curl-up defensive posture of the badger (see Chapter 9).

Fig. 2.4. Boar badger with radio-transmitter attached to a harness. Note the beta-light on top. In all later observations a single collar was used to carry the transmitter under the chin, with the beta-light on top of the neck.

needed something like it, but there was no hope of getting the funds for it at that time. Then, *deus ex machina*, the late Niko Tinbergen, animal behaviourist at Oxford and my professor, friend, and mentor, won the Nobel prize in Physiology and Medicine. In a magnificent gesture, as I was a member of his research team he gave me one-quarter of the prize money to be used as I saw fit. Thus arrived the infrared image intensifier, now more fondly called the 'hot-eye' (Fig. 2.5).

From then on we could actually follow and watch our badgers—not just sit on a platform next to a sett, but go out with a particular animal, watch it feed, and meet other badgers. Peter Mallinson was a master at this, a born naturalist, and both of us spent our nights in the woods, summer and winter, guided by the bleeps of the radio-transmitter and the little green light between the trees. We carried a load of equipment: the hot-eye with a wire to a battery on our backs, a stick to support it when watching animals, the radio-receiver around our necks with a directional aerial held in the hand, earphones over our heads, a torch for emergencies, and a dictaphone to record observations. Fortunately, we rarely met anyone there to enjoy such a spectacle.

In the meantime, while we had been struggling with our technology in the Zoology Department, we had also made some progress in getting other

Fig. 2.5. Night observations using the 'hot-eye', a binocular, electronic image-intensifier system with an infrared searchlight.

results from the badgers themselves. Like the data on sett distribution, these results testified to the animals' behaviour only in an indirect way, but nevertheless they were very important. In my walks around the woods I had noticed the badger latrines, not just next to the sets, but often long distances away. These were assemblages of small pits, sometimes as many as 60 or so together, and many of them had several large badger droppings in them. The whole latrine area often showed signs of vigorous scratching, with clumps of earth and vegetation scattered around; usually there was a clear badger path leading up to it and it was usually in some conspicuous place, such as next to a fence, or a pine tree in an oak wood, or a crossing of paths. I started mapping these latrines and it became quite clear that they were not just spots for defecation; there was no doubt that they served some signalling function, as I had found with hyaena latrines in Africa.

One of the first things we needed to know about the latrines was which badgers used them. Again, a curious train of events led to a technique to tackle this problem, this time starting in Africa. When I worked on the diet of my hyaenas in the Serengeti, several times I had found small, brightly coloured glass beads in their faeces, as well as human hair. The beads had come from the clothes and ornaments of the people of the Masai tribe; the hyaenas had consumed the bodies of the dead (which are left in the bush outside villages) and leather garments decorated with beads. I remembered the coloured glass beads and tried feeding them to badgers by inserting them in pieces of bread, apple, carrot, left next to the setts. I hoped that small coloured sparks would soon brighten up the massive badger droppings in the latrines so that I would be able to trace the animal that produced them. What finally made the technique work was the use of peanuts and bits of coloured plastic instead of glass beads mixed with the peanuts and some treacle. Peter and I cut up sheets of brightly coloured, plastic shopping bags and other things, and every afternoon we fed each badger sett with its own peanut-and-colour mix. Next morning we would find our bits of shopping bag in the badger latrines, often far away, and we could start drawing lines of different colour on our map.

That first map of badger ranges (Fig. 2.6) told a story in itself and it was very exciting to fill in some more gaps every day. Clearly, badgers from most of the setts had an area to themselves, with a distinct boundary separating them from their neighbours. Intriguingly, some of the setts shared their ranges with neighbours.

Then the first results from the badgers with radio-transmitters started to come in, the precious exact data which followed the endless nights of observation (Figs 2.7, 2.8, and 2.9). In the field we were hardly aware, initially, of the way in which these data fitted into the picture that was slowly emerging from our colour markers. But fit in they did, and

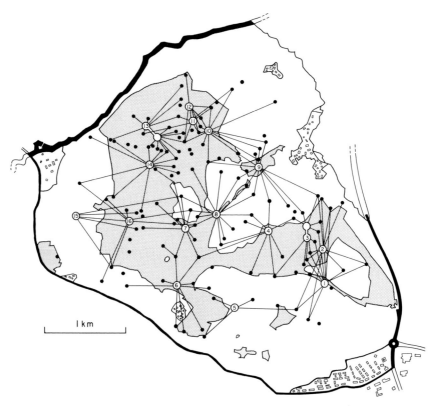

FIG. 2.6. Wytham Woods, with main setts of badgers (open circles), and latrines (black dots). Connecting lines indicate in which latrines colour markers were found which had been fed to badgers on different setts; each number corresponds with a different colour marker (from Kruuk 1978*a*).

beautifully. Most of the latrines turned out to be very close to the edge of the badger ranges, usually well within 50 metres and often used by badgers from either side of the boundary (Fig. 2.10). This meant that our colour-marking technique was an excellent tool for measuring the size of badger ranges. Whichever way we looked at these ranges, with bait-markers or with radio-tracking, they turned out to be surprisingly small: one was only just over 20 hectares (50 acres). Others were bigger, and the average size of a badger range in Wytham Woods was about 80 hectares (or 200 acres; Fig. 2.11).

Let me describe a typical badger watch from those first years of study.

One quiet, damp spring evening, and some time after the sun had gone down, I carefully walked up to one of our setts. The only noises in the wood seemed to come from far away: some cows, a tawny owl, and the rumble of a distant tractor. I tried

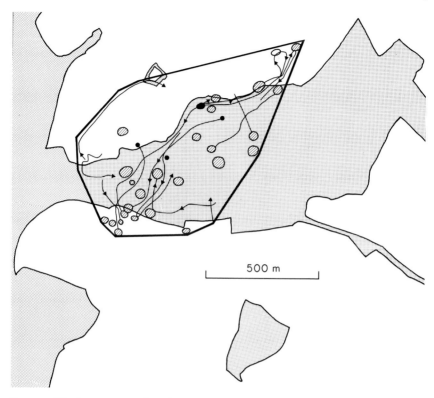

FIG. 2.7. The home range of one female badger in Wytham, as found by radio-tracking. Grey = woodlands, white = agricultural land, black dots = badger setts, hatched area = areas where she fed for prolonged periods (0.5–3 hours), arrows = observed movements, thick line = convex polygon delineating the home range of this individual (from Kruuk 1978a).

to approach without making a noise, so far as that was possible with all the paraphernalia around my neck. Gently I slipped onto the platform we had built in the large oak tree above the Jew's Harp sett, glad to have some time to catch my breath before the hoped-for activity started. The woods were dense there, I felt completely walled in, and it was quite dark before I discerned the first, noiseless black-and-white face moving below me, mercifully unaware of all the heavy science in the tree above it.

The animal was there for a few minutes, then gone, somewhere into the undergrowth. Another followed soon, and another, none of them spending more than a brief pause on the sett; the wood was full of little rustling noises. Then two badgers emerged, almost simultaneously—and one had a beta-light, my target for that night. It was a large boar, one that we had been following for over a month. Ten minutes later I had to unwrap my legs from the uncomfortable platform and follow him as well as I could. Of course, it was quite impossible to go where he went;

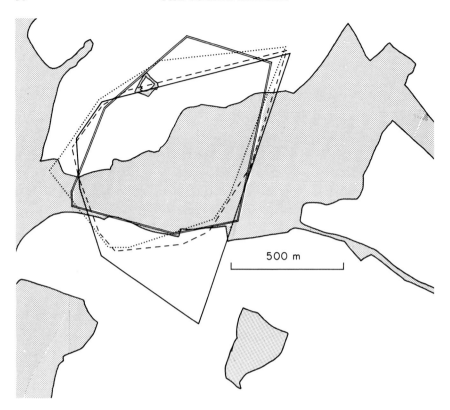

FIG. 2.8. The home range of four badgers from the same clan: two males (full and dotted outlines) and two females (broken and double outlines), including the female from Fig. 2.7 (from Kruuk, 1978a).

the woods were almost inpenetrable even in daytime. As it was, I hoped to anticipate where he went and catch up when he came out at the other side of a patch of bramble, on to a path, into more open country, or on to a field. I concentrated on the radio, waving my directional aerial, deciding whether the signal strength was changing or not, whether the animal was moving or stationary, keeping track of exactly where I was, making sure that the badger did not catch my scent or that of my footprints. It felt like a contest of wits between me and the animal, all in total darkness, and I had to keep on reminding myself that the badger was not aware of it. Once I could see the beta-light all was well again, and I could forget about the radio and watch through the hot-eye.

Fortunately, badgers do not walk very fast, and often, once they start foraging, they stay for a long time in one small area. Twenty minutes after starting off from the sett, I caught up with my animal just as he arrived on the pasture near the top of the hill. He walked quietly, nose low down, gently winding his way across the grass until he stopped and almost effortlessly picked up a huge earthworm, pulling it out,

FIG. 2.9. Clan ranges in part of Wytham Woods. The range of sett 1 consisted of the combined individual ranges as shown in Fig. 2.8, the range of sett 2 was occupied by six males only. The ranges 3 and 4 were used by two females each, and 3 and 4 together were the ranges of two males (full line) (from Kruuk, 1978a).

chewing, and swallowing it within a few seconds. Half a minute later the same thing happened, then again and again. Back and forth through that field he went, picking up scores of worms, ignoring the cows who were ruminating the night away, often less than a few feet distant. Faithfully I recorded the consumption of every earthworm and the timing on to my dictaphone; 90 minutes after the badger started in that pasture, he had eaten 112 worms and nothing else. Then his efficiency appeared to wane, his success decreased, and before I knew it he had left again, unobtrusively slipping into the woods, just after midnight. This time he did not move far; there was a huge, hollow log nearby, a favourite spot of his which I knew of old. The steady bleeps from my radio told me that the badger was obviously curled up inside, doing what any sensible creature should be doing at that time of night.

However, an hour and a half later he was active again, and we were off once more. A repeat of the story, this time in a piece of rather open oak woodland with a lot of dog's mercury in it. He was eating earthworms again, lots of them, slowly

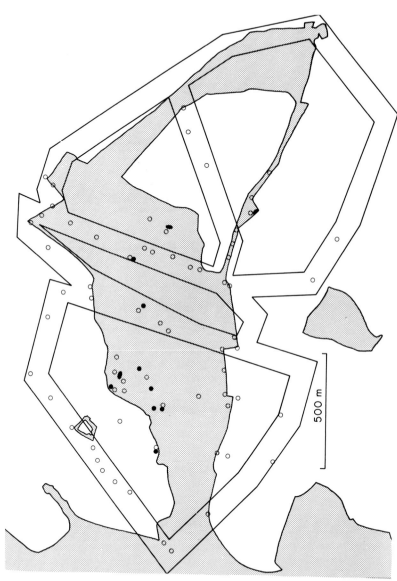

FIG. 2.10. Latrines and boundaries of home ranges. The boundary areas are defined as 50 m on either side of the border (see Fig. 2.9); latrines are open circles, badger setts in black. Most latrines are in the boundary zone, but there are few where boundaries do not run along a neighbouring badger territory (from Kruuk 1978a).

500 m

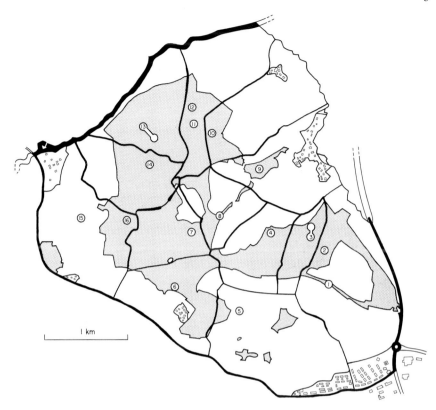

FIG. 2.11. The home ranges of badger clans in Wytham Woods, as determined by the combined results of radio-tracking, food marker recoveries, and the mapping of badger paths. Thick lines: clan boundary defined by a badger path; thin line: exact border position inferred (from Kruuk 1978a).

walking back and forth in the same patch. At four o'clock that morning he returned again to his sett.

Essentially, this was how the Wytham badgers moved about their range and what we found as their main food. Earthworms were their staple diet, mostly obtained in relatively small patches of pasture and in some parts of the wood. There were masses of worms, but what I thought was most important was that they were not always so readily available, at least not in all parts of the range. Some nights provided good worming in one pasture, other nights somewhere else. It looked as if badgers needed all parts of their range just to keep abreast of changes on the earthworm front. I felt that this might be crucial in deciding the size of a badger's living space.

Ideas were beginning to form, ideas which needed testing. At the same time we began to see a little more of the badgers' social life and that too appeared to be relevant to our main question. Some animals in a sett were dominant over others; some sows had cubs, others did not. Some badgers, especially the large dominant ones, always lived in the main sett, whereas others would often stay in small outlying holes in the range (Fig. 2.12). We saw badgers fight in really ferocious encounters on the borders of their area, and there was no doubt in my mind that these ranges were proper territories, defended and marked. There was therefore a structure within the badger clans and a territorial organization between them which, I felt, was likely to be related, somehow, to the way in which these animals exploited their range.

That, more or less, was as far as I got in Wytham. Three years after the badger study started our professor and head of the animal behaviour research group, Niko Tinbergen, retired and our research unit at the University was wound up. I moved to Scotland, while Peter Mallinson continued with badger research for the Ministry of Agriculture. My Wytham period was over; it had been a tremendous experience, with all the excitements of discovery in that gentle, attractive, English countryside. I am writing about it here mostly because those Wytham badgers prompted the questions which I tried to answer in Scotland. When I started badger research in Oxford my main aim was to find out why these animals lived in

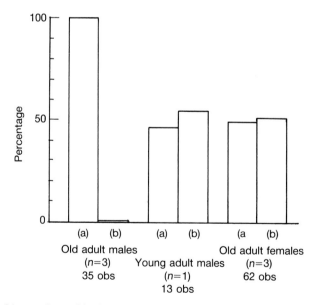

FIG. 2.12. Observations of badgers with radio-transmitters sleeping in main setts or outliers: (a) in main setts, (b) in outliers. Large dominant males are less likely to sleep in outliers than younger males or than females.

groups. During that study the question was tightened up considerably, sharpened, and became intertwined with the problems of population limitation. Badgers somehow exploit their resources in such a way that they can afford to have others living with them in the same area. I wondered how that worked and what the advantages and disadvantages were of living that way.

We had some ideas about the answers, some hypotheses, and we had some of the methods to study these questions, but no more. Scotland offered the opportunity to test possible explanations, to find out what caused differences between populations. The key was a crucial observation in Wytham: some badgers lived in large ranges, others in small ones, and there were large differences in the size of their groups. If that variation could be explained we would know something about the needs and limits of populations, but at the same time we would also answer my first question: why do badgers live in clans?

Inevitably, the Wytham study had done more than just sharpen our wits about gregarious living—it had opened up many more questions about a fascinating species, all directly related to the main problem. I wanted to know how badgers were organized within the clans, i.e. what their social behaviour was like. And related to this social organization, it appeared that badger communication was complicated, including an olfactory network of information. It was important to find out what was happening and how this scent communication could work. Did the black-and-white face-masks contribute anything to their social way of life? and was this predilection of Wytham badgers for earthworms just a local phenomenon and did it have anything to do with their social system? Were they omnivores or not? In Scotland we were given a unique opportunity to start our badger research with the main objective in mind, as well as a host of lesser questions.

Further details

See Kruuk (1975, 1978a, 1978b). On badgers see Neal (1948); Neal and Harrison (1958). On Wytham Woods see Elton (1966).

3

Aims and methods of the study in Scotland

OBJECTIVES

The crucial questions I set out to answer about badgers in Scotland were: how are the clans of these animals organized, what mechanisms limit the size of the clans and their territories, and how? The answers to these problems should provide an insight into population regulation, as well as into the reasons for living in groups.

To go further, this main objective had to be broken down into a number of specific questions, and the Wytham study provided guidance for this. There, it appeared that food played an important role and we had the first inkling of the importance of resource dispersal. So we broke down our main objective into the following.

1. What exactly do badgers eat?
2. How is this food distributed?
3. How are badgers dispersed in relation to food?
4. How is badger society organized?
5. How do badger clans and populations adapt themselves to changes in the environment?
6. What factors other than food could be important?

The way in which I wanted to look at these questions was basically different from the Wytham study. There, I had been struck by the variation in the size of badger ranges and clans, and for the Scottish study I reasoned that by understanding that variation I would understand the controlling mechanisms themselves. If I knew why the animals in one area needed a very large range, whilst a small one sufficed for badgers somewhere else, and if I knew why some clans had only a few members but others many, I should get some clues about what regulates numbers and social organization. Consequently, I wanted to study badgers in several areas, which were as different from each other as possible—different in terms of landscape, vegetation, or numbers. In Africa that methodology had worked well when

I was studying hyaenas and I speculated that it would do so again for badgers in Scotland.

That then was one approach to the questions, the most important one. The other part of the study involved the use of badgers in captivity, where better control could be had over what happened within a group, where every individual badger was known, and where all interactions could be watched at all times, and over many years. The headquarters for this was the Institute of Terrestrial Ecology in Banchory, in the hills west of Aberdeen, where we established a badger colony in a large enclosure in the birch woods and where we had our offices and laboratories.

Most of the fieldwork was done with the help of others. The actual following and watching of shy and nocturnal animals is something better done alone, with little noise, and without having to consider the movements of one's own companions. The help of other scientists, however, was absolutely crucial, not only for increasing the number of nights that badgers were watched, but also for the organization and moving of equipment and the discussion of problems. I had a tremendous amount of help with every stage of this study, and there were several people who were at least as involved as I in all of this, especially Tim Parish. He helped with the Scottish badger study from the beginning to the end and we published most of its results jointly.

STUDY AREAS

When we started in 1975, we set out in a Land Rover and travelled around many areas of northern Scotland to find suitable study sites for the next few years. We wanted to find about half a dozen places, and we specifically tried not only to find sites where there were lots of badgers, but also to get areas representing different habitats, as long as there were any badgers at all. In fact, we found large areas close to our institute where there were no badgers, though we felt there should have been. That, too, provided us with some interesting information later.

The landscapes of the badger study areas which we finally decided upon (Fig. 3.1) are best appreciated from Plates 4 to 8. Three of them were in the agricultural north-east of Scotland, fairly close to our base. There was much pasture on good soils and the badgers lived in plantations of conifers. These three areas were, in fact, the least exciting study sites, and in two of them we had a lot of trouble with gamekeepers poisoning and snaring our animals. The area near Stonehaven was close to the coast, at a low altitude, with some beech and oak woodland as well as conifer plantations and agriculture, and some pretty, small streams winding their way through. The landowner showed me one of the badger setts, and in doing so left part

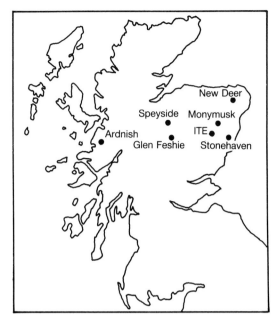

FIG. 3.1. The six study areas in Scotland and the Institute of Terrestrial Ecology (ITE), Banchory. The main study site was in Speyside (Rothiemurchus and Pitypoulish) (from Kruuk and Parish 1977).

of his jacket on some barbed wire—years later it was still there! But whilst he was full of sympathy and interest, his gamekeeper was not, and several times I found badgers which had dragged themselves a long way with a snare around their body and attached to a log, only to die a slow and ghastly death once they got stuck somewhere. Obviously it was impossible to do intensive work under such conditions and we used this area only to obtain data on the badgers' food.

Somewhat similar problems beset our study area near Monymusk, just north of the institute at Banchory. This area was higher up, along a range of hills covered in pine plantations, with only the hill tops still covered with heather moorland. Badgers lived in the belt of plantations and foraged in the pastures lower down. Neighbouring gamekeepers put eggs laced with strychnine on setts, and at least one of our radioed study animals ended up in a snare set for foxes. It was an area of huge stretches of monotonous plantations and rather poor farmland, where few badgers roamed over vast ranges, often passing close to the small farmhouses, and where several people regarded us with suspicion (partly because we often carried large radio aerials and were thought to be checking on TV licences). It was also the area I will always remember as the place where I met one of the ugliest creatures I have ever seen—a completely hairless badger.

Quite different again was the New Deer Forest in the extreme north-east, a very old plantation of spruce owned by the Forestry Commission. This was more or less flat country, the woods being surrounded by the richest farmland in this part of Scotland. Not very exciting, perhaps, but an area rich with the fat of the land. There seemed to be an almost permanent wind, but on the whole the climate was milder than in Monymusk, with less snow in winter. There were some huge badger setts between the spruce trees.

These three eastern areas were important for the study and they yielded much important information. But the really beautiful sites, the areas where nature appeared to have the upper hand, were further west. Two of them— Glen Feshie and Rothiemurchus—were in central northern Scotland, close to Aviemore. Glen Feshie was a typical, spectacular, Scottish Highland glen, a mixture of heather moorland with pine and birch surrounded by high hills and densely populated with red deer. The winters were long and cold, with snow falling for up to 110 days per year; there were a few poor pastures with cattle and sheep lower down the glen, but apart from these the impact of civilization appeared to be small. Badgers were few and far between and they were harassed by gamekeepers—the results from that study area were thin over several years, but enough to tell us what the animals were eating.

In contrast the other study area nearby in Speyside proper, the Rothiemurchus–Pityoulish area, turned out to be our most important one, a site where for six years we tracked badgers intensively and where we got to know almost every tree and most of the badgers. It was at a lower altitude than Glen Feshie and extended from the River Spey into the foothills of the Cairngorm mountains. The 12 km² of the actual study area stretched over two large private estates and included pastures and arable land, a beautiful loch and steep hillsides with birch wood and junipers, and a few pine plantations. It was considerably colder there than on the east coast and was mostly sheep-farming country with rather poor pasture, interspaced with barley fields and turnips as well as woods, dominated by the hills and the river on either side, dotted with old oaks and birches, the loch central to it all. It was a near perfect division between man and nature. In this area we had the use of a small part of a barn, a bothy, which had formerly housed itinerant farmworkers through the varying seasons. It was a dark and damp place, but somehow we grew fond of it. Many ideas saw the light of day there and many a dram was downed next to the old stove. That area, too, had its share of problems with people, but they were easier to overcome. When we first started badgers ransacked a hen coop, and because we were involved with the badgers we were held responsible. So we paid for the hens and that was the end of it. However, right at the end of our study, just before I wrote this book, the same thing happened again, but this time I left the owner of the hens irate by refusing to pay again.

Our last study site was an area on the west coast, just south of Skye. This was the place I loved most of all, less important than Rothiemurchus in Speyside, at least in the contribution it made to our study, but infinitely more impressive. The Ardnish peninsula was miles away from human habitation, its 12 km² used only by sheep and badgers, otters, foxes, roe- and red deer, wild cat, eagles, raven, full of wildlife, surrounded by most spectacular scenery. The climate was wet and mild, with snow rarely falling and its sad, dramatic remoteness was emphasized by the ruins of a small village, Peanmeanach, once inhabited by a small crofting and fishing community but now totally abandoned. There was no road, so we walked or came in by boat to a small house that had once belonged to a shepherd and which we made more or less inhabitable. There were large cliffs on the steep slopes, with patches of dense oak and birch woodland, patches of natural grassland, bogs, and heather moorland, small lochs and several burns, sandy beaches. Altogether I spent about a year and a half there, usually with my colleague Ray Hewson who was studying foxes and their impact on the sheep on the peninsula.

There were not many badgers in Ardnish and those that were there behaved quite peculiarly. First, they did not live in the large conventional setts which I knew from England; they spent most of their time under huge boulders or in small, single holes in the most inaccessible places in that rough country. Second, the badgers themselves looked quite unlike badgers elsewhere; they were smaller and quite a few of them had pink noses. They faced an environment which was fundamentally different as far as food was concerned. I will describe their fascinating ecological differences in detail in Chapter 5.

METHODS

In this group of study areas we tried to answer those first major questions. To start with, we familiarized ourselves with all these areas and spent many weeks getting to know every badger sett, latrine, path, the way around the area at night, the local people, anything that might be significant. Next, we began to collect information on the badgers' diet and on the availability of their food. The methods we used will be described in the next chapter, on the badger diet; but here I want to discuss in some detail the other techniques we used to answer our questions.

It was absolutely necessary and essential to catch badgers, in order to answer our questions, including the problem of how they forage. Catching badgers is more of a skill than a science; to secure a large animal like a badger without hurting or upsetting it too much involves fieldcraft at its best, and I must admit to finding it rather thrilling to get the better of such a fairly formidable adversary. It is necessary to be somewhat ambivalent about it; obviously, the badgers did suffer some distress, even if only because they were in close proximity with their greatest enemy—man. Interfering with them was like fingering something very delicate, far-fetched as that might sound in describing my dealings with such big animals. Because of that, and despite the satisfaction I derived from outwitting them, I would rather have done without trapping. Anyway, it was a necessity for the study and it had to be done.

In Wytham I had caught badgers in stopped snares which were checked at midnight and early in the morning. Getting the animal out of the snare was a rather rough process involving distress both to the badger and captor. So in Scotland we decided on some fundamental changes, namely to catch them in a roomy cage-trap and handle them as little as possible before they were anaesthetized. The trap was made of weld-mesh, about 150 cm × 90 cm and 70 cm high, and usually placed somewhere near to a sett or a latrine, right next to a badger path. The animals were inordinately fond of peanuts and when strewn across the badger path and into the trap this delicacy gave us a lure which was apparently very difficult to resist. On entering the cage the animal would walk into an inconspicuous piece of string stretched across the trap; another piece of string tied onto this first one pulled a nail from the top of the cage which held up the door. The door, hinged at the top, would then fall into place and a couple of catches at the bottom would keep it in position despite any determined efforts by the captive to escape.

This of course was the theory. In practice, badgers escaped or stopped short of the release string, or the trap would be set off by a sheep or a rabbit, or the peanuts would be eaten by mice, and so on. Nevertheless, after the main teething troubles were cured the traps worked amazingly effectively. In spring we achieved a catching success of 30 to 40 per cent, i.e. three or four out of ten traps caught a badger each night. In summer this figure was lower, more of the order of 15 per cent, and in autumn it used to increase again.

Often, when we inspected the traps in the early morning, we would find the badger fast asleep in the corner, having dug up everything within reach in its attempts to escape. To handle the animal we had to immobilize it, and for that we injected 2 millilitres of an anaesthetic called Ketamine. When we got close to the badger it was usually very lively and so the injection had to be given from a distance. For this we used a blow-pipe which was nothing more than a length of narrow plastic gas-pipe (Fig. 3.2). This technique

FIG. 3.2. Badger in a box-trap. Tim Parish darts the animal, using a blow-pipe.

worked wonders. The dart we used was a flying syringe with a needle with an opening along its side. This opening was normally covered with a short plastic sleeve, so no fluid could escape until the sleeve was pushed back. The syringe was filled with 2 ml of the drug; behind the plunger pressure was maintained by a small quantity of gas (lighter-fluid). A red woolly 'tail' on the syringe helped it fly true when blown from the pipe. When the dart hit the badger, preferably in the muscles of the thigh, the sleeve on the needle was pushed back, exposing the small hole and allowing the drug to escape from the dart; the gas pressure depressed the plunger and pushed the Ketamine into the badger. Many things could go wrong with this dart and our blow-pipe technique, but if all went well the animal would doze off about four minutes after being hit. One characteristic of the drug we used was that it was almost impossible to give a badger an overdose; it was perfectly safe and it never caused any fatalities.

Once we could handle the badger we weighed it and described its tooth wear, any injuries, and other characteristics; but most important, and first of all, we checked to see whether we knew the animal from previous encounters. Every animal we caught was tattooed with a number on the hairless skin in the loins. It was a permanent mark that in no way interfered with the badger and was ideal from that point of view; the only disadvantage was that the mark could not be seen when the animal was observed in the field. We tried several methods of marking badgers, including ear tags and freeze-branding, in order to recognize them through binoculars but to no avail; in the end we limited ourselves to tattooing.

The radio-transmitter, with its battery and aerial embedded in resin, was made in our own institute. Nowadays such transmitters can be bought commercially, but we found it very useful to have them tailor-made by John Morris, our electronics expert. They were somewhat smaller than half the volume of a human fist and weighed about 2 per cent of a badger's body weight. In Wytham we had put it onto a harness and attached it to the badger on top of its shoulders. A harness can easily rub in the animals' axillae, however, and we felt that the badgers were never quite comfortable with it. Peter Mallinson discovered that, despite the fact that a badger's neck is wider than its head, a collar can stay on without discomfort if it is fitted snugly around the neck immediately under the chin. In our Scottish studies we followed that design and the radio was carried by the badger under its chin. On top of the collar, just behind the head, we put a 'beta-light', as we had done in Wytham, to produce the greenish glowing spot which we could follow in the dark. The whole attachment could be slipped on very quickly, but it took us some time to learn how to put it on securely, and initially several badgers shed their collar within a day. Later, fortunately, that no longer happened.

Finally, many of the badgers we caught received an injection of zinc-65, a radio-isotope also used in human medicine, in a carefully calculated dose. This in fact was one of our most important innovations, because it enabled us to estimate the numbers of badgers. As I have explained, it was absolutely vital that we should be able to estimate the numbers of badgers in an area and in any one of the clans. It was a simple requirement, but very difficult to meet. It was not good enough to sit next to a badger sett and count the animals coming out at night, because we knew that many spent the day in often almost inaccessible single holes far away, or they would only emerge very late at night, or they would go into one hole and come out of another in a confusing mêlée. And, of course, this sort of problem is exacerbated with a nocturnal animal. However, we hit on the idea of using the badger's faeces: they were easy to find and there were many of them.

Our idea was that if we could recognize faeces from particular individuals, then the *proportion* of recognizable faeces should give us an indication of the total number of badgers in that population. For instance, if there were three recognizable badgers in one clan and if we then found that half of the faeces from that area came from these recognizable animals, we could estimate that there were, probably, six badgers in that clan. To recognize our badgers for this purpose, therefore, we used the isotope zinc-65, which could be detected in the faeces by a scintillation counter that measured the radiation (Fig. 3.3). It was sometimes difficult to distinguish the small dose we gave the badgers from the large amount of natural radiation from the granite in Scotland. But for about two months after a badger had been injected this was not really a problem.

The technique was simple and in fact worked very well. Nevertheless, we had to check it in experiments with our nine captive badgers, in the large enclosure at the Institute, to see whether it was feasible (Fig. 3.4). We also used the technique in wild badger groups where we knew the numbers, since we had spent so much time with all the individuals in the groups that direct counting actually did work. We received much valuable help from Dr Martyn Gorman, of Aberdeen University, and the technique became established as routine. In fact, we used the isotope-labelled badger faeces for several other purposes, for instance to find out which badgers were actually defecating on the territory boundaries and which ones did it close to the setts. The main purpose of the isotope, however, was to estimate numbers.

After half an hour a captured badger, fitted with collar, tattooed, and injected with zinc-65, would begin to come round from the anaesthetic. It would sway its head and gradually begin to make attempts at controlled movement. It would never try to bite, only struggle; at that stage, we would put it back into the nearest badger sett, inside a hole, if necessary covering it with some bracken or branches and making sure that it did not wake up when we were there. The next night it would be foraging again in its range,

Fig. 3.3. Tim Roper using a scintillation counter to check for the presence of faeces containing the isotope zinc-65 in a badger latrine, Speyside.

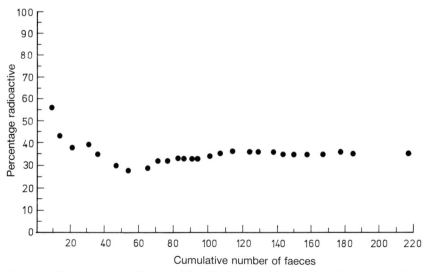

Fig. 3.4. The percentage of faeces with radio-isotope, from a group of six badgers in an enclosure of which two had been injected with zinc. Faeces were collected daily. The figure shows that at least 80 droppings have to be collected before a reliable estimate (i.e. that one-third of the badger population was injected) could be made (from Kruuk *et al.* 1980).

carrying its radio-collar as if it always had; and if it came anywhere near a trap, the chances were that it would follow the trail of peanuts and walk in again.

The radio-transmitter on the animal would send out a signal, a very short bleep, of about one a second, which we could pick up with our receivers. Ideally, the transmitter would function for about eight months and during this time the bleeps could be heard up to five kilometres (three miles) away by our highly sensitive receivers. Even if the badger was deep inside a sett, the radio-signal would reveal its location up to a mile away.

The essential point about radio-location is the detection of the direction from which a signal comes, using the precise directional aerial which we carried around when watching the badgers. As a standard routine we went out in a Land Rover with a big aerial on top that could be rotated (Fig. 3.5). Each badger-transmitter operated on a different radio-frequency; we selected which badger we wanted to find, tuned in, and obtained a bearing with the aerial from a couple of directions to tell us approximately where the animal was. Then we would move in on foot with a smaller hand-held aerial to bring us into close contact (Fig. 3.6).

For each badger which we radio-tracked we made a map, just as I had done in Wytham (Fig. 2.7), and when we had finished with an animal we

Fig. 3.5. Land Rover with rotating directional aerial radio-tracking badgers in Speyside.

would draw a line, a convex polygon, around all the observations. The enclosed area was the badger's home range over that period. We had noticed that a badger did not immediately visit its whole home range in the first few nights after we started following it; in fact, almost every night the known range for a radio-badger would increase. This would continue up to a certain point, usually within two weeks, then the curve would reach a plateau (Fig. 3.7) and that asymptote would indicate the home range. In later observations we used the number of grid-squares in which we observed a badger as a measure of range size. Both methods have advantages and disadvantages, but it would take far too long to discuss them here.

In principle, we would use the radio-tracking device to enable us to watch the animal, to see what it was doing and where, if the surroundings of the badger permitted. It is perhaps more usual to employ radio-tracking to put dots on a map, to describe the range of an animal with triangulation, and there are some fully automated radio-tracking stations in use which feed location data directly into a computer. These systems cut out the cumbersome process of actually watching animals, with full automation the acme of scientific achievement. I have never been really tempted by this

FIG. 3.6. Tim Parish with radio-receiver and directional hand aerial, radio-tracking badgers at night.

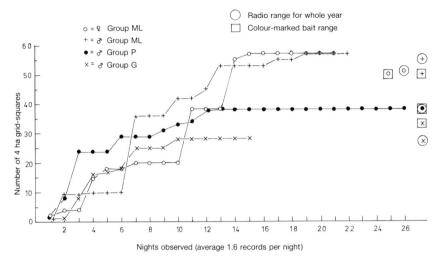

FIG. 3.7. The size of some known badgers' home ranges, compared with the number of observations. The figure shows that animals should be observed over at least two weeks before the full range can be estimated (from Parish and Kruuk 1982).

technology; I am sure that there were times when it could have been usefully employed in the badger study, but there is no substitute for direct observation. The events missed when relying on just radio-signals, the ideas generated when watching the animals themselves—all these fully justify the extra effort needed to keep up personally with the badgers. And apart from all that, I feel that actually watching animals in their own environment is one of the greatest satisfactions biologists can derive from their studies.

Further details

See Parish and Kruuk (1982); Kruuk et al. (1980); Kruuk and Parish (1977, 1982, 1987); Kruuk (1986); Parish (1980). See also Cheeseman and Mallinson (1980); Amlaner and Macdonald (1980); Macdonald (1983).

4

Food and available resources

THE NEED FOR A STUDY OF FOOD

If there had been elephants in Europe it is likely that, sooner or later, they would have turned up as an item in a badger's diet. The list of food remains found in badger faeces is virtually endless. There is an excellent thesis on badger diet in Sweden written by Skoog (1970); for Britain Neal devotes over 40 pages to the different foods in each of his later books (1977, 1986); and there are many scientific papers on the subject. The question for me was whether there would be any point in adding to all of this by studying the food in our own areas. With so many other pressing problems, would it still be worth while to increase the already lengthy list of published data on diet?

If 'food of carnivores' *per se* were our main subject, the answer to that question would have to be in the negative; we have enough data on that topic. But to me, food was only the beginning of the story. I had to relate the diet to other aspects of the badgers' environment and I needed to know exactly what these animals fed on in our particular areas. It was essential to have this information before going further to look at how and where food was available and how that could affect the badgers' behaviour, foraging, social organization, and populations; none of these aspects had been examined before. This was therefore my excuse for adding even more to the inventory of the badger diet. Furthermore, with hindsight, it was good that we did, because the picture that emerged was fundamentally different from that we had been shown previously, namely the picture of an opportunist eating everything available.

There were no distortions of the truth in the previous publications on diet (with the exception of one early paper, of which Skoog showed that the author had just made up his data), but when the composition of an animal's diet is discussed, a great deal depends on the way in which the data are presented, as I will show further on.

THE METHOD OF DIET ANALYSIS

To get accurate and detailed information on what a nocturnal animal eats there is usually no alternative to faecal analysis. Most field studies on mammals seem to resort to this and there is a risk that it becomes an end in itself. However, I think that we did not fall into that trap—but that was not for the want of opportunity, for we collected a large amount of material. In the end we had analysed well over 4000 droppings.

Every two months throughout the year we collected the scats we needed in all the study areas, usually from near the badger setts themselves and usually 20 per area, although we collected 50 from our main area in Speyside. At times we had to struggle to get a decent sized sample, because, especially in the droughts of midsummer and the snows of midwinter, faeces were difficult to find; however, in spring and autumn there was no problem.

Over the years we became adept at finding scats, which could be quite difficult to detect, even when we knew exactly where the badger setts were. In most, but not all, places there was a well-used 'latrine' within a few metres of the sett entrances, and we used to start our collections at these sett latrines because we could be sure about which animals had visited them. But to get a full sample we often had to go further afield, collecting from known latrine sites and always on the look out for new ones. The trouble was that badgers defecated either on their own sett latrines, or on latrines exactly on the territorial boundary with their neighbours, which meant that we could not know from which of the two clan ranges the faeces came; there were few latrines scattered inside the range itself. The latrines also played a very important role in the territorial behaviour of the animals, and I will say more about this in Chapters 6 and 9.

After we collected the faeces in polythene bags, they were deep-frozen for later analysis, or sometimes salted if no freezer was available. Later, in the laboratory, each dropping was washed through a sieve and the rinsing water caught in a large beaker. The solids in it were allowed to settle, then some were collected in a pipette and examined under a microscope. What we were seeking with this particular procedure were earthworm chaetae, the tiny bristles of which each worm has about 1000 (Fig. 4.1). The rest of the dropping in the sieve was thoroughly rinsed, then dropped in water in a large shallow tray so that we could easily identify all the contents and count them. Wads of hair, bits of barley, skins of pignut tubers, shiny pieces of beetle, skins of leatherjackets (larvae of the daddy longlegs)—a great variety always turned up. Especially common were the very transparent gizzard-rings of earthworms, which we had to stain to make them show up properly; each worm has just a single ring, so they were very useful for quantifying worm-remains (Fig. 4.2).

The problem came just at that particular point; how to quantify everything. Identification was not so difficult; we made up a reference collection of hairs, feathers, various insects, fruits, something which took some time to bring together, but which was immensely useful for

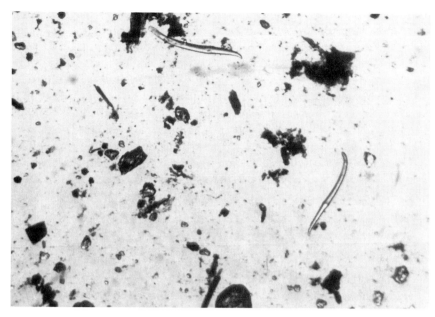

FIG. 4.1. Chaetae of the earthworm *Lumbricus terrestris* under the microscope. Each bristle measures approximately 1 mm; one worm carries about 1000.

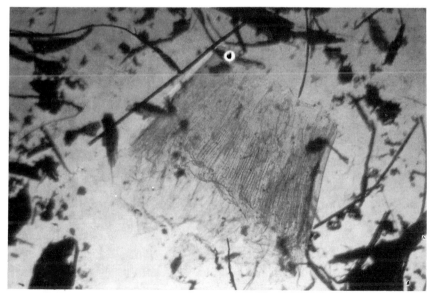

FIG. 4.2. Gizzard ring of earthworm. It is highly transparent and there is only one per worm; the largest gizzard rings measure approximately 0.5 cm in diameter.

comparison with the remains which had passed through the badgers. It was after identification that the problems really started: comparing quantities of foods is something which has beset faecal analyses in many other species of animal. The most obvious difficulty was the fact that for some kinds of prey many more remains show up in the faeces than for others. For instance, small mammals have relatively more hair than large ones and difficulties might arise when comparing the remains of invertebrates (beetles, earthworms) with vegetable food or mammals. If we wanted to present something more than a list of food items, therefore, we had to calculate correction factors, or estimate in some other way the quantities of food from what we found in the droppings. Of course, we could still use the lists of food items and record the frequency with which they occurred. This method is the one most often used in the literature, but it gives a biased picture if we try to interpret how the frequencies of food items in the faeces translate into actual diet. Nevertheless, frequency lists are very useful, for instance when we compare diets of animals from different areas or at different times.

With the badger food analysis in the Scottish studies we took a rather diverse approach. First, we calculated the 'frequency of occurrence', which I have just maligned, i.e. the percentage of droppings in which prey items occur. In general, this tends to overemphasize smaller prey and underestimate the more abundant ones (because the remains of several prey of the same species within one dropping will usually be counted as one). Next, we also estimated for each dropping the *relative volume* of each prey item in the corresponding food intake—not the volume in the scat, but the volume which that prey item would have taken up in the actual meals of the badger which had resulted in that dropping. Therefore one scat containing the remains of 25 earthworms and 10 small beetles, and nothing else, could rate as approximately 95 per cent volume earthworm and 5 per cent beetle, although the beetles were much more prominent.

We then plotted the mean volume of earthworms, for instance, for only those faeces in which earthworms were present, against the frequency of occurrence of that prey species. This gives the overall importance of the food item in the badgers' diet, and the figure indicates immediately whether this importance is due to a food item being taken more or less frequently, or in smaller or larger quantities. It would of course be better still if we could calculate the calorific values of different kinds of food, rather than merely presenting relative volume. That will have to wait for a further study, however.

There is one more important snag to all faecal (and stomach) analysis that is rarely taken into consideration. It is a difficulty which we, too, had more or less to ignore: the problem is caused by the fact that at some times of year the animals eat more than at others. Faecal output varies accordingly, but usually, when we evaluate results in the laboratory, we assume that the amount of faeces produced per day does not vary significantly. The consequences of this can be quite important, as just one example may show. In winter a badger eats very little and often nothing for weeks or more. Thus the odd carcass of a small bird that it might eat during that time may be half its food intake for several days. When calculating the diet of badgers for the whole year we take the proportion of birds in the diet in each winter month and add it to the percentage found in the summer months to produce a figure for the importance of birds in the diet over the whole year. Clearly, this overemphasizes the importance of food items taken at those times when badgers eat little, and it undervalues food from times of plenty, which is equally wrong. We can only allow for this type of bias by taking into account the actual quantity of food eaten by the animals at all times, but this is rarely possible.

Perhaps the message from all this is that a great deal of scope remains for further refinements of methodology in diet analysis and also, that care must be exercised in the interpretation of results whatever the method chosen. Nevertheless, even with the customary crude approach in the use of faecal analysis we can get a good overall impression of the diet of a species, and most work on carnivore food relies heavily on the dissection of the scat.

BADGER DIET: RESULTS

Despite all the potential problems of interpretation, there was one phenomenon in which the results from the badger scat analyses were quite unambiguous, and this was to me the most striking conclusion of this part of our work: in all the different Scottish study areas, be they highland or lowland, forest or pasture or moor, badgers were highly specialized single-minded earthworm consumers. Whichever way we analysed the results, earthworms figured prominently, with the characteristic chaetae and gizzard rings present in almost every scat and usually in large quantities (Table 4.1, Fig. 4.3). There were also many other foods and the table gives a good idea of the badgers' catholic tastes. In fact, the list of items in the Scottish badger diet is not too different from that found by other workers in England and in various other countries in north-western Europe.

The diet is graphically presented in a different form in Fig. 4.4, which shows not only how often a food category was found in the faeces, but also the estimated volume whenever it occurred. Rabbits, for instance, were found in only 15 per cent of the scats, but when they were present they constituted almost 60 per cent of the volume of food corresponding with those scats, so overall the volume of rabbits in the badger diet was 60 per cent of 15, i.e. 9 per cent. Figure 4.4 shows at a glance that earthworms were

TABLE 4.1. Contents of 2159 badger faeces from six areas in Scotland. The first column shows the percentage of all scats containing a particular food category and the second column shows the estimated relative volume of this category in the badger food

Prey species	Percentage occurrence in faeces	Percentage volume in diet
Earthworms	97.5	53.8
Snails	0.8	0.04
Insects		
Tipulid larvae	24.6	1.0
Caterpillars	6.3	0.3
Beetle larvae	5.5	0.2
Beetles < 1 cm	62.7	2.1
Beetles > 1 cm	41.4	1.6
Bumblebees	6.1	0.8
Wasps	0.4	0.1
Others	0.6	0.03
Fish		
Salmon	0.3	0.1
Amphibia		
Frogs and toads	5.5	1.7
Birds		
Woodpigeon	2.1	0.8
Passerines	0.2	0.08
Others or unidentified	6.6	1.5
Rodents		
Voles	3.5	1.5
Others or unidentified	2.1	0.5
Lagomorphs (rabbit)	14.6	8.6
Large mammal (carrion)		
Sheep	2.4	0.4
Deer	1.1	0.2
Others or unidentified	0.3	0.07
Vegetable		
Oats	25.7	6.4
Barley	4.1	1.6
Rowan berry	1.9	0.8
Acorn	4.5	1.3
Unidentified fruits	0.6	0.06
Pignut (*Conopodium*)	36.0	5.3
Other roots	0.2	0.02
Fungi	13.2	1.5
Other or unidentified foods	0.1	0.01
Leaves (incidental, probably not food)	93.9	9.1

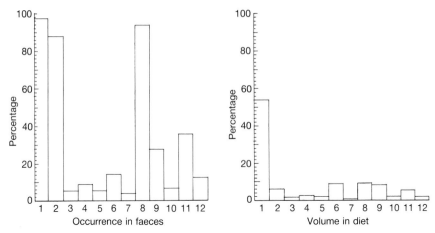

FIG. 4.3. Histogram showing (left) the frequency with which different kinds of food items were found in badger faeces from all the study areas, and (right) the volume which we estimated these kinds of food to occupy in the actual diet of the animals (from Kruuk and Parish 1981). 1 = earthworms, 2 = insects, 3 = amphibia, 4 = birds, 5 = small mammals, 6 = rabbits, 7 = carrion (except rabbits and birds), 8 = leaves (probably accidental), 9 = cereals, 10 = fruits, 11 = pignuts, 12 = fungi.

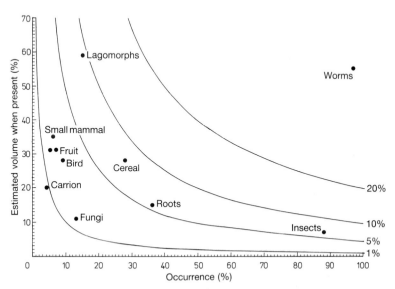

FIG. 4.4. The diet of badgers in Scotland: the volume of foods whenever they were present in the diet against the frequency with which they were taken. The curved lines (isopleths) connect points of equal overall importance in the total diet (in terms of volume) (from Kruuk and Parish 1981).

taken almost always, and in large quantities, whereas insects, for instance, were eaten very often but only in small volume, so that their overall contribution to the diet was rather similar to that of the rabbits. Clearly, earthworms stand out from the others.

We compared the badger diet from the different study areas in a similar way; Fig. 4.5 shows some of the main foods. What is most interesting in the figure is the fact that the points for each kind of food, from the various areas, are so close together, showing basically how similar the diets were. However, the figure does not show of course that some of these foods were not eaten at all in some of the sites (for instance, there were no rabbits and no cereals in Ardnish). Nevertheless, the figure does demonstrate, for instance, that prey like rabbits were rather variable in their occurrence in the diet, but the volume in which they occurred was more constant. Similarly, pignuts—the tubers from the small, white, umbellifer flowers which cover northern grasslands in June—were taken much more frequently in some places, but in each scat they occurred in more or less the same quantities.

Figure 4.5 should be viewed against the background of our different study areas in Scotland, with their huge variety of landscapes: the acid moorlands or rich agricultural pastures, the highland birch woods in the

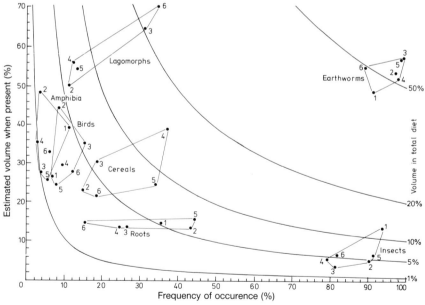

FIG. 4.5. Food of badgers in different study areas, expressed as in Fig. 4.4 (from Kruuk and Parish 1981). Areas: 1 = Ardnish, 2 = Glen Feshie, 3 = Monymusk, 4 = New Deer, 5 = Speyside, 6 = Stonehaven.

hills, or the flat, lowland conifer plantations. We could not escape the conclusion that badgers were earthworm specialists, because wherever they fed they seemed to be able to find worms in huge quantities. Yet, at least in theory, it might be possible that somehow the appearance of these areas was deceptive, that badgers simply ate anything they could get hold of, and that all these areas happened to be crawling with worms. There was only one way to find out and that was to estimate the different food availabilities. I will discuss this later in this chapter.

The time of year is likely to be a very important factor in the availability of food for the badger. We did indeed see that some foods were eaten at all times of year, but others only during particular seasons. It was important to find out exactly what was happening, because one of my main questions was whether any of these resources could have an effect on badger populations. If such an effect operated only during a particular period of the year it could be very important, but it could also remain hidden if we looked only at annual averages.

Figure 4.6 shows what badgers were eating over each two-monthly collecting period taken separately and combined for all the areas. Clearly, foods like fruit (mostly rowan berries), cereals, and frogs were highly seasonal, but earthworms were not and were taken at all times. Insects were more complicated: we frequently found them in badger scats throughout the year, but in summer badgers picked up much higher quantities whenever they ate insects. Just to make sure, I calculated whether badgers in the various study areas did the same thing, and indeed for each food the seasonality or lack thereof was nicely synchronized throughout Scotland. It was possible to calculate the extent of this seasonality, i.e. to estimate how large this annual variation was for each kind of food. As Fig. 4.7 suggests, fruit is by far the most variable food that badgers take, followed by cereals, then frogs, fungi, and various others. The least variable, most reliable food is indisputably earthworms.

All the food items taken by badgers were very small in size and many of them were elusive in some way or other. Their acquisition, however, required no stalking, running, nor indeed any other special catching technique. Obviously, earthworms were the linchpin of badger foraging, whichever way they got them. They dominated the diet at all times, everywhere, and I think that the realization of their importance was one of the main results of this part of the study. Worms had been mentioned in several earlier studies of badger scats, but their key role had never been properly quantified. Not surprising, perhaps, because worm remains almost disappear in the heaps of remains of cereals, pieces of insect, and rabbit fur. Once we recognized the crucial importance of earthworms, many aspects of the badgers' ecology and behaviour fell into place.

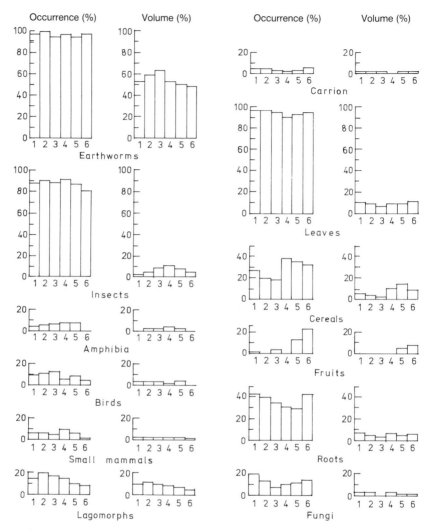

FIG. 4.6. Food of badgers in all areas together, at different times of year.
1 = January–February, 2 = March–April, etc. (from Kruuk and Parish 1981).

However, scientists never seem to be able to state things categorically and there are always some qualifying remarks. In the case of the badger diet, I have to put things in a somewhat more international perspective: the importance of worms in some other countries is minimal. Scotland may be quite representative for north-western Europe, but earthworms are scarce in, for instance, the Mediterranean countries, and no large animal could possibly survive there living almost exclusively on earthworms. In northern

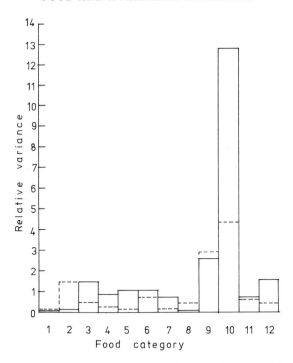

FIG. 4.7. The variability of different kinds of food in the diet of the badger. The histogram indicates how variable the food is between two-month periods; broken lines = volume, full lines = frequency of occurrence (from Kruuk and Parish 1981). 1 = earthworms, 2 = insects, 3 = amphibia, 4 = birds, 5 = small mammals, 6 = rabbits, 7 = carrion (except rabbits and birds), 8 = leaves (probably accidental), 9 = cereals, 10 = fruits, 11 = pignuts, 12 = fungi.

Italy I found badgers eating some worms in summer, when they could find them in the alpine meadows, but in winter those meadows were inaccessible because of snow. There the badgers ate mostly fruit, especially olives, which are available almost the whole year. Of course they also took insects, slugs, and birds, but many more fruits, including figs, cherries, plums, grapes, and others. These were not wild fruits but cultivated agricultural products and they appeared to take the place in the badgers' diet there that is occupied by worms in Scotland (Fig. 4.8). Thus, there too badgers were specialists, but on a different food.

AVAILABILITY OF FOOD AND THE
BEHAVIOUR OF EARTHWORMS

Back in Scotland, the badgers' feeding habits forced me to look in some detail at earthworm behaviour and ecology. Interesting, perhaps, and all

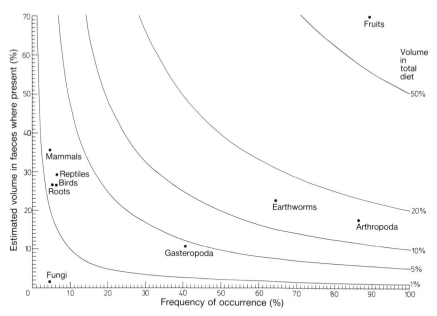

FIG. 4.8. The diet of badgers on Monte Baldo, in northern Italy, presented in the same way as the diet of Scottish badgers in Fig. 4.4 (from Kruuk and de Kock 1981).

very useful to an understanding of badger diet, but often I felt that the study of earthworms led me further away from actual badger behaviour than I was prepared to go: it was also far from easy. The worms were highly nocturnal, inaccessible in daytime, especially active during wet nights, and even then difficult to find and catch. Purely subjectively, I would have preferred to study the availability of food species of Italian badgers more closely. In our Scottish study areas we had to assess not just earthworms but also other potential food sources. As an example of how this was done I will describe some of the relevant fieldwork on the numbers of rabbits.

One afternoon I battled my way slowly through a thick, young plantation of pine trees in our study area near the east coast of Scotland, near Stonehaven. With clip board in my hand and pine needles down my neck, I had to go down on my knees to read the map. Up a slope, down a little gully; not being able to see more than a few feet on either side, it took me well over 20 minutes to finish just one square of one hectare. In that particular place the density class of rabbit holes was 2, which in our code meant that there were between 11 and 25 per hectare.

On to the next grid-square, which was partly in the plantation, partly pasture. Density class 4 there, which meant between 51 and 100 per hectare. The next square was open pasture: no rabbit holes. Three square kilometres were sampled that way in Stonehaven, 300 grid-squares of one hectare; there were more rabbit holes in that badger site than in any other. Every study area was covered in this way, fortunately with the help of several dauntless students, so that in the end we could rank the areas for rabbit abundance. There was a clear pattern: the further west in Scotland, the fewer the numbers of rabbits, and in Ardnish, on the west coast, there were none. The Scottish north-east is good, rich, agricultural land, but it becomes more impoverished further west—we know now that it is not just rabbits that are thin on the ground there, but also mountain hares, grouse, and many other species show a similar pattern.

In theory rabbit holes may not be a very precise indicator of numbers of rabbits, because in some places one animal may use several holes, especially if there is sandy soil for easy digging; elsewhere, rabbits may hardly go underground at all. Nevertheless, the number of rabbit holes gives an overall impression of the population and, most importantly, we found a very good correlation between the density of rabbit holes and the number of rabbit carcasses lying about (usually they had died of myxomatosis). Of course, those rabbit carcasses were potential badger food.

What we were trying to do was to get some idea of the *differences* in the availability of an important food supply between study areas. We realized that it would be impossible to measure accurately what this availability would be in absolute terms. Even if we could count every single rabbit, it would still be impossible to know whether these rabbits would be potential prey: some would be impossible for a badger to get, others easy (e.g. those with myxomatosis). So *absolute* availability was a pipe-dream, but *relative* availability was something that could be estimated. Furthermore, it made a fascinating comparison with the badger food in these places.

Figure 4.9(a) shows one of the results of this exercise in estimating rabbits, comparing the average number of holes in an area with the frequency with which we found rabbit fur in the badger droppings. There are two points to be made from this graph: first, it was clear that badgers responded to the presence of more rabbits by eating more of them; second, some of our areas had enormous numbers of rabbits (an average of 20 active holes per hectare is a very high density) yet badgers did not eat correspondingly enormous numbers of them.

Rabbits were just one of the badger foods that we looked at in this way. We also mapped fields of barley and oats, and patches of pignuts, as well as carrion (such as sheep and deer carcasses), rowan trees, and marshes with frogs. As I showed before, none of these foods were really very important to badgers; they ate them, more in one place than in another, as a soupçon rather than a main course. For all these different foods the story is very similar to that of the rabbits: the more there is in an area, the more badgers will consume. I have plotted some of these results in Figs 4.9(a)–(c). If the results had all been as they were for these minor foods, the overall conclusion would have been simply that badgers eat whatever they can find in their patch—true opportunists.

However, when we look at earthworms, the badgers' main food, the simple picture that we found for the other items in the diet is completely upset. The measurement of density and availability of earthworms is a story in itself, and because of the importance of worms to badgers I will go into this in some detail.

There are more than 20 different species of earthworm in Britain. Many of these live in very specific habitats, such as dung piles, acid bogs, and particular kinds of leaf litter. But there are several species which live in pastures or in woodland soils, and of these the large 'night crawler' *Lumbricus terrestris* is by far the most important in terms of biomass. It has

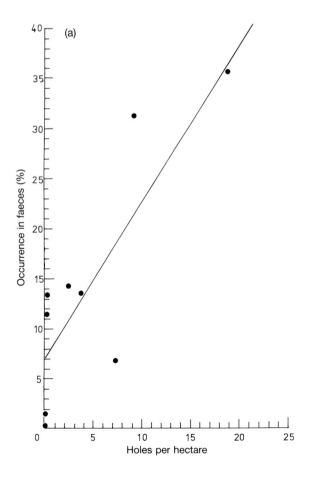

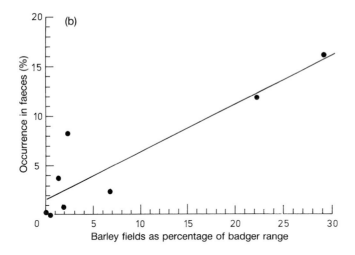

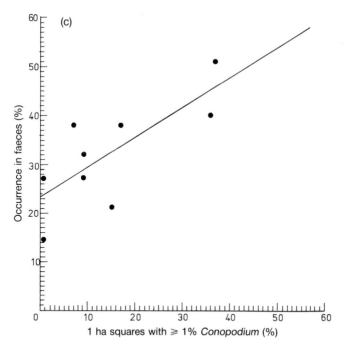

FIG. 4.9. The density in which various badger foods occurred in different study areas or parts of areas, compared with the occurrence of those foods in the faeces of badgers there (a) Rabbits, (b) barley, (c) pignuts (*Conopodium majus*). All correlations are statistically significant.

permanent burrows which go vertically down from the surface, sometimes as deep as one metre; with one or several entrances. It is a large animal as worms go, rarely weighing more than 10 grams and up to 30 cm long, but usually about 5 grams in weight. It often feeds on the surface around its burrow, not just by crawling around, but by holding on to the sides of the burrow with its tail end, whilst the front part of the body moves around, grasping pieces of vegetation which are then pulled inside. The worm is able to hold on to its burrow with the help of the chaetae, minute bristles, eight on each segment, about 1000 in all, with a very characteristic shape. This hold on the sides of the burrow is very strong indeed and if we, or badgers, pull at the front end the worm will break rather than let go—that is, unless it is done properly: there are ways of getting the worm out whole.

Worms may also eat entirely undergound, consuming earth and internally removing the edible organic matter. Therefore *Lumbricus terrestris* is not wholly dependent on feeding on vegetation on the surface, but when conditions are right, it will do so. In fact it and one other species (*Lumbricus rubellus*) are the only earthworms to forage on the surface in substantial numbers—but only at night, during the right kind of weather, and when the right plants are available. When we took a sample of 50 earthworms, half from pasture and half from arable land, those from arable land all had guts full of earth, whilst 13 of the 25 from pasture contained fresh leaves (mostly grass). This of course is where the story becomes important for badgers, because they have to catch their worms on the surface. In fact, even if badgers could dig efficiently enough to find earthworms underground, most of the night crawlers would be able to slide down their tunnels, and do so incredibly fast. They have to be caught on the surface and surprised in such a way that they do not break nor have enough time to withdraw into their tunnels.

The questions then are: where are these earthworms present in the soil, and when and where can they be caught on the surface? I will start with the last, more behavioural question. Every countryman knows that worms come out at night and are always associated with rain. But there is more to it: they can also be found for several nights after rain has fallen, when the grass and soil are still damp, and it has been shown that temperature is important. In short, night crawlers are most likely to be abroad when it is pitch dark, the temperature around 10°C, and during or within two days of the last rainfall. Moreover, even when there has not been any rain for some time, worms may still come out as long as there is a good dew. This last possibility means that often there are places, fields or patches of woodland, where many worms are on the surface during nights when neighbouring fields are devoid of such signs of life, because dewfall is often very localized.

Unfortunately, dewfall is difficult to measure, at least on a scale large enough to be of use in our badger study. The point about worms and dewfall is important, however, and I will come back to it later when I discuss the size of badger territories. For the purpose of comparing worm availability between areas we will have to forget about dew and just look at rainfall and temperature. On the basis of our own and other researchers' observations on earthworms, we coined the term 'worm night', a somewhat arbitrary description of the kind of night when worms would be on the surface, that is a temperature never below 2°C and a rainfall of at least 2 mm over the preceding 3 days.

The purpose of this worm-night criterion was to be able to compare different regions for their suitability for catching earthworms and also to compare this suitability at different times of year. There are several possible objections to our definition of worm night. For instance, it is a measure for whole nights and weather may alter dramatically during one night; if there had been a brief frost it could not be called a worm night, even if the temperature at midnight had gone up to 10°C and the surface was alive with worms. Also, the wind was not taken into account and worms avoid emerging when it is windy. Despite these flaws, I think that the number of worm nights for a place or a time of year gives a reasonable idea about the relative suitability for earthworms on the surface.

In Fig. 4.10 the average number of worm nights per month for two of our

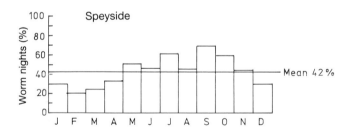

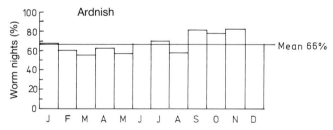

FIG. 4.10. The percentage of nights suitable for catching earthworms on the surface, over all the months in a five-year period in Speyside and in Ardnish (west coast) (from Kruuk and Parish 1981).

study areas (Speyside in the central Highlands and Ardnish on the west coast) are compared over a five-year period. All our study areas were rather similar to Speyside, but Ardnish was much wetter and less cold. In Speyside and all the other areas there was an average of only 45 per cent of nights which could be classified as worm nights; also in all these areas there were much larger seasonal differences than on the west coast. For instance, in Speyside, for more than one-third of the whole year in winter fewer than one night in three was a worm night; but from May to October there were plenty of worm nights.

We also had to assess what numbers of worms were present underground in the area. This was something we could measure directly during the day by using an ingenious method developed by earthworm specialists— pouring formalin over the soil. The procedure is that a square of 50 cm × 50 cm is marked out, sprinkled with a highly diluted solution of formalin from an ordinary watering can, and the number of worms which come to the surface counted in the following 20 minutes. We had to do about a thousand of such samples, which amounted to well over 160 hours of watching worms come to the surface (we usually did two plots simultaneously), or about one whole week of solidly staring at the ground, if we had done all samples consecutively.

The first thing that struck us was the huge numbers brought to the surface. Densities of over 30 large *Lumbricus terrestris* per metre square were not uncommon on the east coast, and then there might be another 20 or more *L. rubellus* and about another 15 of other species. Since then I have learned that as a rule of thumb a farmer reckons to have about the same biomass of worms in a field as the biomass of cattle he can graze there. To me, this kind of quantity was quite amazing and I still find it astonishing that we, or any other organism for that matter, do not make more use of this huge earthworm resource. During the Second World War a project was started in England to investigate earthworms as a source of protein for human consumption and a paper was published in *Nature* which analysed the chemical composition of worms. The general conclusion was that the overall composition did not differ substantially from prime beef. Probably mere prejudice stops us from utilizing this resource as well as, perhaps, the difficulties of harvesting such a crop.

The very large numbers of worms were found only on agricultural land, at least in our Scottish study areas. I know that elsewhere similar numbers can occur in woodland with oak, ash, or sycamore. Ardnish, our west coast area, had no *L. terrestris* at all, but large numbers of *L. rubellus* instead. This difference in worm species appeared to have a large effect on the badgers' foraging behaviour (Chapter 5). In our other areas pastures were the best places in which to find worms (Fig. 4.11), next came arable fields, and last

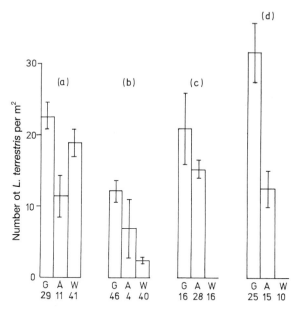

FIG. 4.11. Earthworm densities in grassland (G), arable land (A), and woods (W) in (a) Wytham, (b) Speyside, (c) New Deer, and (d) Monymusk. The woods in (a) were mixed deciduous, in (b) birch, and in (c) and (d) coniferous (from Kruuk *et al.* 1979).

and least were the woodlands, which were usually conifer plantations although there was much birch wood in Speyside.

In our areas we knew the earthworm densities and under what weather conditions they would be on the surface. There is a further important point: badgers can only catch worms efficiently on short grass (less than five centimetres long) or on more or less bare ground (Chapter 5), so short-grass pasture is the ideal worm-catching ground for a badger. This is where the high densities are, where worms would feed on the surface instead of underground, and this is where badgers can catch them easily.

It would have been easier if I had been able simply to estimate earthworm availability without having to go into all the detail of worm biology. The problem was that it was very difficult actually to observe or measure how many earthworms were present on the surface, in different places, at the time that badgers were foraging. We had to resort to indirect means to try and understand worms sufficiently so that we could predict their availability.

THE RELATION BETWEEN DIET AND FOOD AVAILABILITY

At the beginning of this section I showed that as far as rabbits, cereals, fruits, and other minor foods were concerned, badgers were almost perfect opportunists: when there was more, they would take more. For earthworms, the story turned out to be quite different. In all our areas we compared the badger diet with worm numbers, with the biomass of worms in the soil, and took into account the number of rainfall days, the number of 'worm days', the amount of pasture, the area of short-grass pasture, the total area of agricultural land, and all these in various combinations. The important conclusion was that none of this had the slightest effect on badger diet: we could find no relation between the relative quantities of worms which badgers consumed and populations, or availability, of earthworms in their feeding areas. In all areas badgers had a more or less similar proportion of earthworms in their food, whilst quite enormous differences were found in worm populations and in the various indicators of worm availability.

At first this result was difficult to understand, but then we realized that it was consistent with what should be expected of a food specialist. It meant that badgers would always, somehow, obtain their earthworms, and if there were fewer worms, they would either eat less overall or change their foraging to compensate for it.

So far I have discussed differences in food and feeding between our study areas. There were also differences between *seasons* within those areas which were equally important. In Fig. 4.10 I showed that summer was a much more favourable time than winter and early spring for catching earthworms on the surface. Because *L. terrestris* is a long-lived species (reaching eight or ten years of age), we may assume that the actual numbers of worms were not much affected by the time of year. Probably earthworm numbers were similar in summer, but catchability was greater; nevertheless, as we have seen, the badgers' diet was consistently high in worms throughout the year. However, other foods appeared to be taken seasonally, as they became available. Rowan trees, for instance, bend under the loads of berries in autumn, at least in some years; that is when we found them in the badger droppings and at no other time. Barley and oats were available before and during the autumn harvest, gleaned from the stubble fields and directly from the heavy ears, but also, by some enterprising badger individuals, in winter from the barns in which the grain was stored.

The pattern of food availability, with the badgers' response to it, taught us a number of important lessons. First, it showed that badgers were quite capable of using a resource whenever or wherever it turned up—the hallmark of the opportunist. Second, however, almost in contradiction to this, earthworms were treated in a special way; somehow, badgers managed to take them in large, similar quantities irrespective of availability. Apparently badgers adjusted their foraging to whatever the worms were doing: if there were few, badgers probably worked harder to get them. Or perhaps badgers only foraged when earthworms were available? I will discuss this further in Chapter 5. Under conditions of really extreme earthworm shortage badgers could, and did, change their diet.

As a general point I think that a comparison between the availability of food and an animal's diet is the only way to decide whether a species, a population, or an individual should be called a specialist or an opportunist. It deserves the specialist label if it eats more of a particular source than can be expected on the basis of availability and should be called an opportunist (within a certain range of foods) if intake is correlated with availability. Badgers in Scotland somehow manage to be both.

Let me add one final remark of caution about badger food. In all our discussions about badger diet, I have only talked about the *relative* importance of various foods, not about *absolute* quantities. The main reason for this is that with faecal analysis we were not able to measure the food intake, only the diet in terms of relative importance of different foods. We know that badgers eat far less in winter than in autumn, which is an important aspect of their ecology. So we have to say that for instance worms were eaten in the same *proportion* the whole year through, yet we know that the actual *quantities* varied tremendously. In fact, these actual quantities of worms consumed in various months may well have followed the curve of 'worm nights' in Fig. 4.10, but we have no evidence. Of course, this difficulty does not apply to the comparisons of badger diet between the different study areas. I do not think, therefore, that this methodological problem invalidates the conclusion that in our areas badgers were earthworm specialists using other resources opportunistically.

Further details

See Kruuk and Parish (1981); Kruuk and de Kock (1981); Kruuk *et al.* (1979); Brown (1983); Leitch and Kruuk (1986). On badger food see Neal (1977, 1986); Skoog (1970); Andersen (1955); Paget and Middleton (1974); Ciampalini and Lovari (1985); Mouches (1981). On earthworms see Edwards and Lofty (1977); Macdonald (1983); Satchell (1967); Kollmannsperger (1955); Lawrence and Miller (1945).

5

Foraging behaviour

CATCHING EARTHWORMS

An observation in our study area in Speyside.

June 1978, about midnight, in a pasture next to the birchwood. There is little moon, the grass is dripping wet with dew. Cattle are lying down in a corner of the field and I am standing near the edge, watching through the 'hot-eye'. Totally oblivious, the old, radio-collared female slowly moves across the grass, silently, nose close to the ground. The animal stops and picks up something. An earthworm is pulled out quickly, without any conspicuous movement, then immediately snapped up with a slight upward and sideward flick of the head. No pause, the badger goes on again, same direction, same speed. Half a minute later I see another strike; this time, the worm manages to get a better hold of the side of its burrow, and it takes the badger several seconds before the prey is pulled clear, slowly, without breaking, then snapped up.

Once we knew what badgers were eating and what was available to them and where, it was important to discover exactly how they set about acquiring their food. For this we used observations such as the one I have just described. We needed to know the badgers' behaviour in detail to understand why some foods were taken opportunistically and others such as worms almost regardless of availability. It was necessary to understand the strategies with which badgers exploit their resources in order to study whether feeding had anything to do with their peculiar territorial and group organization.

The observation described above was typical of badger foraging and could be seen in badgers anywhere in Britain or north-western Europe, as long as some means of watching them in the dark was available. There seems to be little effort involved on the part of the badger, no digging, running, or pouncing; the animal behaved as if it were grazing (Fig. 5.1). Almost always the earthworms were pulled out of the ground, rather than merely picked up, but the effort appeared comparable to pulling a blade of grass. Mostly, though not always, the worm did not even break; when I looked through the chewed and broken up remains of earthworms in the stomachs of two badgers that had been killed on a road in Oxfordshire, I found 148 heads and 110 tails. This suggested that the tail end had broken off in only 26 per cent of the badgers' prey.

Fig. 5.1. Typical posture of badger feeding on earthworms.

The distance between two successive worm captures in a field could be as little as 20 cm, but usually it was several metres. Characteristically, the badger walked without making many sharp changes of direction; it tended to stay in the same field or part of a field by moving in approximately the same direction until it reached the edge or some other point, where it turned back again, often covering more or less the same ground. In this manner a badger would stay in the same small patch for periods of up to two hours. During that time, in an average pasture in Scotland, it would catch worms at a rate of 2.7 per minute ($\pm$0.8 standard error, calculated from 198 worm captures between April and September). We weighed a large number of *Lumbricus terrestris* which we caught on the surface at night and found an average weight of 5.5 grams. This meant that a badger caught on average $2.7 \times 5.5 \times 60 = 890$ grams per hour, which was just about its total requirement per day. Usually, the success rate of badgers went down quite markedly in the last few minutes before they left their patch, either because the numbers of worms on the surface decreased, or because the predators were satiated (Figs 5.2 and 5.3).

When I watched these animals at night, it struck me that they found worms only right under their muzzle. This observation could be important, because it could indicate a restriction on the way in which a badger could use its habitat. So I decided to do some experiments to determine exactly what was happening. Our captive badgers at the Institute in Banchory were as keen on earthworms as were their wild relatives, so we gave them the

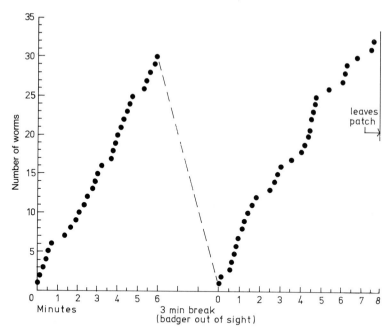

Fig. 5.2. Numbers of earthworms caught by a badger in Wytham, feeding on short-grass pasture. Note very high feeding rate, slowing down at the end of the observation (from Kruuk 1978*b*).

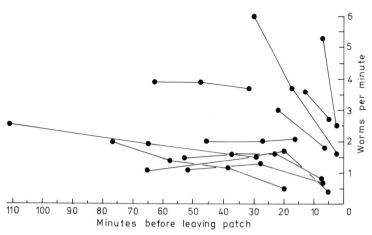

Fig. 5.3. Feeding rates of badgers in Wytham, catching earthworms in 'worm patches' on short-grass pasture. Feeding rates were rather constant within each observation, slowing down towards the end (from Kruuk 1978*b*).

opportunity to catch worms on grass swards with different lengths of grass. This sounds easy, but the earthworms gave us trouble, as might be expected. They crawled off at the first opportunity and since we had to put them out on the grass well before the badgers arrived on the scene, they needed restraining. We tied them, with thin cotton thread, to match-sticks pushed into the ground; that kept the worms perfectly still on the grass and looked, to us at least, exactly as if they were feeding on the surface at night.

We tried several different lengths of grass. In that experimental set-up we found that when the grass was about 2 cm long badgers caught, on average, about six worms per minute, and if it were 20 cm long they would catch only one and a half worms per minute. Of course, the situation was contrived and artificial, with an extremely high badger utilization and worm density, but I think that that did not matter too much; the experiment demonstrated the principle that was operating. In those experiments the capture rate of 2.7 worms per minute, which I had seen in the wild, would be obtained with a calculated length of grass of just over 5 cm. If the grass was longer than that, the whole process quickly became less efficient.

It was difficult for badgers to detect worms when the grass was long. Moreover, the reactions of free-living worms to disturbance also made their capture in long grass less likely; as soon as a worm was disturbed it would swiftly withdraw into its burrow. Clearly, these were the reasons why we saw badgers foraging on short-grass pasture, or on patches of grazed short grass in pastures with mixed lengths of grass. For instance, when we watched four radio-collared animals on pasture for 19 hours altogether, they spent 99 per cent of their time on grass shorter than 5 cm, although the grass was as short as that in less than half (45 per cent) of the fields there; so the animals had a highly significant preference for short grass (Fig. 5.4).

As I mentioned, when a badger was hunting worms it would generally remain in a relatively small area, often less than a hectare, for a long period before it moved elsewhere to feed. An animal would do this even when there were masses of earthworms to be found everywhere else, but there were also times and places when badgers would walk long distances to catch their worms, picking up other food as they went (Fig. 5.5). In Wytham woods, I had noticed that during damp nights when worms were abundant on the surface almost 90 per cent of my observations of foraging badgers were of animals which stayed in one small area (for at least half an hour in less than one hectare) *patch-feeding*, as described above. During dry nights, however, i.e. 'non-worm nights', only 25 per cent were patch-feeding (Figs 5.6 and 5.7), an indication therefore that foraging behaviour changed quite dramatically when earthworms were thin on the ground. Our Scottish badgers did much the same.

There were also other indications that badgers adapted their foraging to

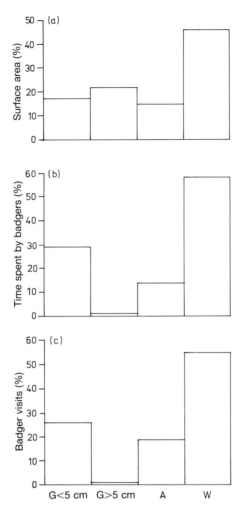

FIG. 5.4. Badgers feeding in different parts of their ranges: G < 5 cm = short grass, G > 5 cm = long grass, A = arable land, W = deciduous woodland. (a) Area of the range covered by these vegetations, (b) percentage of time badgers spent there (out of 63 hours), (c) percentage of badger visits to these vegetations (*n* = 77) (from Kruuk *et al*. 1979).

earthworm abundance. For instance, in one badger territory in our area in Speyside we had four pastures, all grazed intensively by sheep. Two of these were rather poor with a worm density of just under 10 *Lumbricus* per square metre, whilst the other two had well over 20 earthworms per square metre. In all other aspects, such as length of grass, proximity to setts, woods, etc., they appeared very similar. Badgers spent 30 per cent of 46 hours of

FIG. 5.5. Badger in a typical foraging walk, often used for covering long distances.

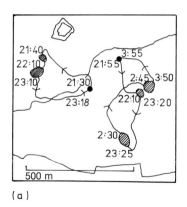

(a)

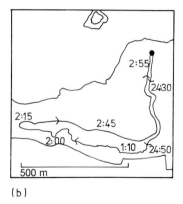

(b)

FIG. 5.6. (a) Movements of one badger during two successive nights with wet weather: 'patch feeding'. The central area is woodland; hatched area = feeding patch; black dots = setts. (b) Movements of one badger during a night with dry weather: 'long-distance feeding' (from Kruuk 1978b).

observation in the worm-rich fields and only 6 per cent in the poorer ones.

During the dry times of the year, in the middle of summer, badgers might also use another technique of catching worms, aimed at species of earthworm other than *Lumbricus terrestris*. These species congregated in or under cowpats, especially under those that were one or two weeks old and not yet completely dry. The badgers would demolish them with their long claws and dig small pits around or under them. One cowpat could hold 30 worms or more, but most of these were only very small ones. An area where

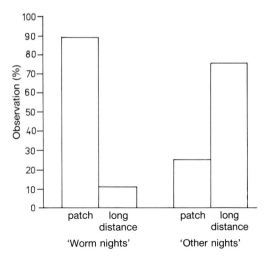

FIG. 5.7. Observations of badgers feeding in 'patches' (at least half an hour in less than 1 hectare) during worm nights ($n=63$) and during other nights ($n=48$; $\chi^2=44.2$, $p<0.001$).

cattle had left a lot of cowpats over a few weeks could look like a battlefield when badgers had been feeding there for a night or two. During such dry spells badgers are also known to dig up garden lawns or other rich pieces of soil to catch earthworms, but in a way quite different from their normal 'search and pull' strategy.

There was good evidence, therefore, that badgers did change their foraging behaviour with changes in earthworm availability. How much this affected their actual foraging effort in terms of energy expended, we do not know. However, as we have seen in the previous chapter, the result was that the relative importance of earthworms in the diet was kept rather constant and very high. Badgers also adjusted their foraging behaviour to worm availability by foraging less, overall, when fewer earthworms were catchable; this happened especially in winter, but perhaps also over shorter time-spans in other seasons. They can build up large quantities of body-fat to see them through lean times.

OTHER FOODS

Barley (or oats) was easiest to obtain for badgers whilst still on the stalk, just before it was cut and harvested. The animals would never eat cereals before they were quite ripe, so in fact the cereal season would have been very short for them were it not for some aspects of the farming system that enabled them to get hold of barley at almost all times of year, at least in our main study area in Speyside. I will first describe the simple foraging for cereals in the fields.

What was very striking about the badgers' 'harvest' was that they would eat cereals only in a very small part of a field, an area often no larger than 10 m × 20 m (Fig. 5.8). The fields were large expanses of food, literally tons of barley over several hectares, and night after night badgers would eat in the same spot, not necessarily near a sett and not necessarily at the edge (though usually fairly close). A badger would move little for an hour or more, quietly pulling down stalks by wrapping a foreleg around a bundle, then putting its weight on the stalks, and biting away at the barley ears.

FIG. 5.8. Oat field after a badger spent several hours feeding. Note stalks pulled down in bundles.

Some ears would be bitten off in the process, but most would be left on the stalk, with the badger eating the grains and the spikelets. If a few badgers did this in the same place for a few nights, the result was quite obvious. Also, other animals made use of the patches of flattened vegetation, especially woodpigeons and rooks, but also roe-deer; between them they could do a great deal of damage. Even so, it always looked worse than it was; when I calculated the actual yield of that area as a percentage of the total yield of the field it was only a minute proportion. I should add, however, that at times badger cubs made quite a mess in fields when playing. In the days before the combine harvester that also meant loss of yield, but nowadays technology can take this kind of damage in its stride.

Oats were tremendously popular with the badgers and if there was an oatfield nearby all barley would be ignored (but not many oats were grown in our study areas). In the New Deer area there were some fields with wheat and this was also highly preferred over barley, which was not surprising, since the barley ear is well protected by its long, sharp spikelets. In other countries there are often complaints of badger damage to maize, but this crop is not to be found in Scotland. In all these cases badgers almost always ate in particular spots, small areas in the fields, rather than roaming randomly about each field, or eating just from the periphery.

In our Speyside area the barley grain was stored, often for several months, in a big heap inside an old barn. It was an open invitation to badgers and there were nights when three or four, small, green beta-lights could be seen bobbing up and down in the pitch dark. With the hot-eye we could distinguish every detail of the badgers, sitting right in or next to the barley, munching audibly, paying scant attention to each other or anything else that might be going on.

That was one source of barley which often lasted to the end of the winter and into spring; another was the supplementary feed for cattle in the fields or on the hills. Scottish cattle are very hardy, especially the pure or cross-bred Highland cattle, and they are left outside throughout the year. But they are provided with extra food, often in the form of crushed barley, and our badgers would often walk directly to the place where the cattle troughs were; we could recognize the crushed barley in their faeces. With this, the stores in the barn, and the regular crop in the fields, barley became very important at almost all times of year. Interestingly, it was almost always taken at just a few small sites.

There are good descriptions in Ernest Neal's (1986) book of how badgers take many of the different foods. But two categories of prey occurred in the badgers' diet so often, next to worms and cereals, that a more detailed description is needed: insects and pignuts. From the faecal analyses we knew that insects were taken frequently at all times of year but only in small quantities; they included bumblebees and wasps (both taken from nests), as well as beetles of all sizes (amongst others, dung beetles and carabid beetles), but most important were leatherjackets and caterpillars. Leatherjackets are the larvae of Tipulids (daddy longlegs), which live in the ground, consume the roots of grass and other plants, and are often to be found in the grass matt or in the top layer of soil between roots. The caterpillars which badgers eat also live in almost the same places; they are the larvae of Noctuid moths such as the yellow underwing, also root eaters. These larvae, like most of the other kinds of food, were picked up by the badgers almost everywhere, and I never had any indication that the animals concentrated on them; they were common titbits, eaten wherever badgers came across them.

Pignuts provide an excellent example of a typical badger food and the way in which it is exploited. *Conopodium majus*, an umbellifer, has pretty, small, white flowers and each plant has a small tuber, which was the part that the badgers ate.

Another field observation.

An evening in late May 1981, just after dark. One of the males of the Sheilich clan has just left the main sett, and walks down the high bank, under some huge oak trees. Sometimes I can hardly see him, because of the tall grass, but fortunately the beta-light keeps on betraying him. Close to the Sheilich Burn, 10 minutes after leaving the sett, he is right in the middle of a large patch of pignuts, with the flowers like a snowshower around him. Yesterday he did exactly the same thing, so I expect him to stay where he is now, probably for the next hour or so. I take off all my radio equipment, leave it behind a tree so I am less encumbered, and very quietly I walk close to the animal, taking care to stay well down wind. Every step takes several seconds, as I have to make sure that I don't hit any branches, and that I keep myself against a background of trees. Closer and closer, and after a few minutes I am only six metres away; through the hot-eye I can see every detail, with the badger totally oblivious to my presence.

The animal walks a couple of paces, nose close to the ground, then digs again, fast, with both front legs, nose inside the hole that he makes. Two or three seconds, then he picks up a small delicacy, the head goes up, the pignut is crunched up, with chewing and smacking noises. Three paces, the animal digs again, bits of grass flying up, the badger changing position twice, a deeper hole this time. Tearing through the soil and roots; success again, chewing noises.

Over the next 20 minutes the animal never stops, steadily meandering around about five square metres, churning up the surface, with a hunting success of about five pignuts per minute. Then his rate slows down, not surprisingly: I would guess that his stomach is full with pignuts. Suddenly, he turns round and walks off, at the usual, steady pace: I have to get back to my radio again, to try and keep up with him in the darkness.

Pignuts constitute about 5 per cent of the annual diet of Scottish badgers but as much as 14 per cent in the summer, in our study area in Speyside, so they can be fairly important. They are quite nutritious, though small. We sent them for analysis to the ITE laboratory in Merlewood, England, and they were found to contain about 19 per cent starch, 2 per cent protein, and 0.5 per cent fat. They are also nice to eat, with a pleasantly nutty, sharp flavour. Pignuts occur on dry, open, natural grassland, in rough, permanent pasture as well as along the banks of the burns, roadside verges, and steep grassy slopes between fields. In soft, fertile soil the tuber could be 8 cm deep or more, but badgers never bothered with those; the deepest pit they dug in their search for pignuts was 6 cm (average 2.9 cm). Perhaps this was the reason why the deep pignuts were also the biggest—up to 7.5 grams—and longer lived, having escaped the badgers' claws. The result of the pignuts' distribution and the depths of the tubers in different soils, was that badgers dug for them in rather confined areas—another clearly patchy supply of food.

We saw badgers stalk rabbits near their warrens (rather like a dog or a fox), or dig out rabbit nests; we saw them eating the carcasses of sheep and deer, tearing them to bits and making a mess as no other carnivore does (at least in Britain); and we saw many other kinds of food being taken. The one thing that most of these various food categories have in common is that they provide large quantities for badgers to eat in fairly small areas. I will argue later that this *patchy* supply of food is of fundamental importance for their social organization.

EXPERIMENTS ON FORAGING BEHAVIOUR

When thinking about these 'patches' of food, of worms or whatever, we always wondered how badgers recognized them as such. We cannot actually see a food patch, and often I only recognised it for what it was from the behaviour of the badgers. To find out more about the mechanism of patch-feeding, we created artificial food patches for the wild badgers by distributing small piles of a few peanuts in a hectare of short grass in our Speyside study area. I thought that if we could watch the behaviour of badgers in a field where we knew the distribution of food exactly, it would provide us with a clue about their food-finding strategy, especially with respect to earthworms. I had already noticed that captive badgers in our enclosure at the institute in Banchory found peanuts in very much the same way as they did earthworms, i.e. only when they were immediately under their noses.

The experimental field was divided into squares with sides of 2 metres, with numbers on the corners that could be seen from a hide. Each square might, or might not, have peanuts in the centre. Badgers learned very quickly that that field meant food, although there had not been any natural food there before. They came to it from a long way away, although they could not possibly have smelt the peanuts (in fact they also came on nights when we did not have peanuts out), so they must have remembered the location of the field from landscape features, after having found the peanuts for the first time by accident. Once they were in the field, however, something more complicated happened. They walked through it, more or less in a straight line, then started to search around immediately after they had found one peanut. If we put peanuts in the squares on one side of the field only, badgers would very quickly discover them with their strategy and stay on that side of the field just by turning around more often after they found food.

These were fascinating observations that told us a great deal about how even a rather large carnivore can use a very simple foraging strategy for most of its requirements. I was fortunate to have the help of Tim Roper from Sussex University, who had come to work with the badgers as a postdoctoral visitor to our group in Scotland and who carried out the peanut experiments. He later continued them in England and published an interesting paper on this work. Observations on many other animals and birds indicate that the badger is by no means alone in this manner of exploiting patches; for instance, there are good studies on this with foxes and with blackbirds.

EARTHWORMS AND WEIGHTS OF BADGERS

It has been known for a long time that badgers are much heavier in winter than in summer. For instance, more than 30 years ago Neal and Harrison found that in southern England females weigh about 9 kg in summer and about 12 kg in winter. The same happens in Scotland, and in Sweden these differences are even more pronounced. In Banchory we found that captive badgers, with constant quantities of food throughout the year, showed the same weight fluctuations. Probably, this is a physiological adaptation to the unreliability and stringencies of winter food: badgers put on weight in the autumn, then reduce their activity through the winter to what is not quite a hibernation, but close to it. Recently, Fowler and Racey (1988) demonstrated in our captive badgers that their body temperature was reduced in winter by several degrees, though not quite as far as in proper hibernators such as hedgehogs or bears.

Badgers in different areas have different weights in summer. They probably have different weights in winter as well, but we did not measure these because of problems in catching them at such a time. In summer, badgers on the Scottish west coast weighed about three-quarters of those from the east coast, with animals from our more central Speyside study area weighing somewhere in between. The greatest difference was between females, with an average west-coast sow weighing about 6.5 kg and one from the east coast almost 10 kg. We related this to the importance of earthworms in the diet in these various regions and the measured earthworm availability in badger habitats. Earthworms might be involved in determining the summer weight of badgers (after all, they were the badgers' staple food), so we looked at the latter in our Speyside study area over a series of years, when we found that the earthworm density was declining drastically and when the badgers' earthworm intake fluctuated as well as declined.

In the study area a change in farming practice had caused a steady deterioration of the grassland, the badgers' chief foraging areas. There was more moss in the grass and the pasture did not look so healthy. Over the eight years that we looked at these areas, we estimated that the density of *Lumbricus terrestris* per square metre declined from 12 to 3 in the northern half and from 7 to 6 in the south. Taking into account changes in the amount of pasture and slight differences in the weather (numbers of worm nights) the worm availability in the Speyside study area fell by 41 per cent. On the other hand, there was more barley, both as a crop and as a supplementary feed for livestock, at most times of year, so badgers had something to fall back on. Nevertheless, we found that badger body-weights in summer fell from about 9 and 10 kg (females and males, respectively) to about 8 and 9 kg, and over the years there was a direct correlation between badger weights and the relative volume of earthworms in their diet in early summer (Fig. 5.9). At the same time it seemed that badgers somehow made

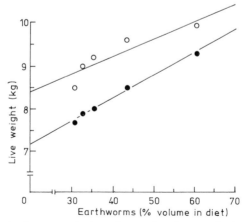

FIG. 5.9. The relation between relative volume of earthworms in the diet and the weight of badgers, from March to June 1977–1981, Speyside. For males $r = 0.89$, $p < 0.05$; for females $r = 0.99$, $p < 0.001$ (from Kruuk and Parish 1983).

up for these bad springs and summers by eating much more barley later on in the year. We found a good negative correlation between volume of worms in the diet in spring and volume of barley in the food in autumn (Fig. 5.10). Thus, in those later years in our study area in Speyside, the badgers appeared to suffer from a lack of earthworms, but they made up for it with an inferior, less preferred food. After a few years of this new regime, the cub-production in the worst affected ranges dropped to zero.

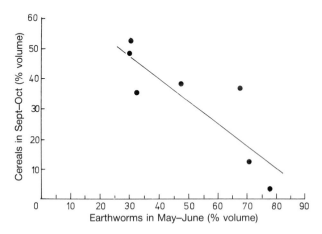

FIG. 5.10. The relation between the volume of earthworms in the diet in early summer and the volume of cereals in the diet in autumn, Speyside, 1976–82 ($r = -0.85, p < 0.05$) (from Kruuk and Parish 1983).

FORAGING ON THE WEST COAST OF SCOTLAND

Because of the enormous effect of farming practices on worm populations, badger food and foraging appears to be based on agriculture and dependent on man. Our observations in the study area in Speyside and in the eastern areas of Scotland bore this out: badgers were almost commensal. I thought it important for comparison to study the animals in a place where the effects of man were probably much smaller, which was the reason why we concentrated on the study area in Ardnish, just south-east of Skye, on the Scottish west coast.

In those remote mountain regions it is almost only the scattered sheep which testify to the presence of man, and the lush pastures which maintain the badger in more civilized parts are unheard of. The comparison revealed some very important points and we obtained some fascinating insights into the badgers' behaviour. Unexpectedly the animals of Ardnish behaved quite differently. As an illustration I will describe a night of radio-tracking on that remote, beautiful west coast.

Night time, after another wet, windy October day. I am perched on a steep, rocky slope, leaning against a small birch tree. Radio, binoculars, as well as hot-eye around my neck, a heavy battery on my back, earphones on my head, a large aerial in the hand, shivering cold. I sit and wait, and have been doing so for the last couple of hours. Finally, just before 10 o'clock, the old badger female with the radio-transmitter emerges from under the huge rock just below me, from the sett where she has spent the day. Alerted by the changing radio signals, I look at her through the hot-eye, watch her dropping down the slope between the boulders, slipping away at a speed which leaves me far behind within a few minutes. I slowly work my way down; it takes all my efforts not to break my bones or equipment. By the time I catch up with the old sow, half an hour later, I come up from down wind, and I can get quite close again. She is perching on a dead sheep, tearing pieces of the shoulder and neck off the carcass, a ewe which has been dead for just over a week. Bits of fleece blow in my direction and she spends a lot of effort pulling off skin. Ten minutes after my arrival she descends to the ground, digs a hole next to the sheep, defecates, scrapes again, sits, scent-marks with a quick squatting movement and she is off again.

   Up the slope again, through bracken and heather, at a steady pace, this time to a rather flat bit of ground about half-way up the hill, almost a third of a mile away. The sheep have kept the grass short there, a patch of natural pasture scattered with bracken. I can only catch frequent glimpses of the badger, but that is enough to deduce what she is doing. She digs a small hole, mostly with only one paw, right next to a heap of sheep droppings. Her nose goes down, smacking noises, she digs a few strokes again, more chewing. Each stop takes only a few seconds, she eats a few small worms, then the badger walks on again, to the next heap of pellets, digs. Over the following two hours the old sow slowly meanders through the bracken, in and out of small grassy patches, and I tally 34 diggings. Somewhat drowsily, I suddenly discover that the signal is not moving any more, and I have not seen her for 10 minutes. She has gone to sleep, in a dense, dry patch of bracken. The time is half past two, and I decide to call it a night. When I find her again, the next day, she is in a different sett, half a mile from where I left her.

The sow in this field observation was a typical west-coast badger, small compared with east-coast animals: she weighed less than 6 kg, whilst an east-coast female would be about 9 kg. Her range was huge, and like other badgers in the area she ate a much greater variety of foods than badgers elsewhere. But what I found especially intriguing was that the animals here would move to a different sett almost every day. For one thing, this meant that I had to spend much more time searching, because I never knew where and when to find them; I was used to homing in on one main sett in a badger territory. There was no doubt that there was an important difference here.

   The Ardnish peninsula was only about 12 square kilometres (5 square miles) but it seemed much bigger because of the high hills. Steep slopes dropped into the sea all around us, with small coastal 'greens' in the valleys, patches of oak and birch woodland interspaced with big cliff faces and large boulders, but everything dominated by heather moorland and bogs. I had selected the area to study badgers, of course, but often I found it difficult not to get distracted by the otters, ravens, eagles, buzzards, deer, seals, and many other species. However, like almost all other areas on the west coast, the peninsula was dominated by sheep, and there was little doubt that it was because of sheep that badgers managed to fare as well as they did.

There were about 800 ewes, in daytime usually fairly low down on and around the coastal greens, at night trekking higher up on the slopes. No doubt they had a considerable effect on the vegetation and on the numbers of earthworms. That is how the badgers were affected, but curiously in a manner quite different from what happened in cattle-grazed eastern Scotland and in England. The reason for the difference was that there was another species of earthworm on the west coast.

The large night crawler *Lumbricus terrestris*, common in pasture land almost everywhere, was absent, perhaps because the soils were too acid. Instead, the closely related *Lumbricus rubellus* was common, again mostly under grass. It was much smaller than *L. terrestris*: whereas an average-size *L. terrestris* picked up from the surface would weigh about 5 grams, *L. rubellus* could only average about 0.3 grams. Second, its habits were different: whilst *L. terrestris* lived quite deep down and tunnelled up to the surface to forage, *L. rubellus* lived close to or almost in the surface vegetation. Furthermore, it did not live just anywhere—it had very clear preferences for particular parts of the natural grasslands.

First, we found the worms on the low-lying coastal greens which were strewn with sheep droppings. Pellets occurred everywhere, without any striking concentrations. In some patches on the greens the wild grasses, *Agrostis* and *Festuca*, were taller than elsewhere, i.e. they were 3–15 cm tall, whereas most places had grass less than 3 cm high. It was those tall grass patches which attracted the worms: when I counted the numbers of *L. rubellus* there (by digging up and sorting patches of soil by hand) I found an average of 224 per m², but the much larger short-grass areas had only 29 per m².

In those coastal greens it made little difference to the worm distribution whether there were sheep droppings or not, presumably because these droppings were so very scattered. But higher up there were small patches of grassland everywhere between the bracken, on the slopes where the sheep spent the night. There sheep pellets occurred in accumulations—clear heaps—and were very attractive to *L. rubellus*: from my samples I calculated that worm density per square metre amounted to 356 immediately next to sheep droppings, compared with 93 elsewhere. Those areas higher up, incidentally, had almost no really short grass.

At night the Ardnish worms were to be found on and in the grass, just like the night crawlers elsewhere, at least if the weather was wet (which it was, more often than not). On dry nights the worms were still very close to the surface, or just under the turf, and were easy to catch by a badger scratching the surface. From this it seemed rather obvious that a badger should search for worms on the surface when the grass was wet and dig for them just below the surface when it was dry, working in the tall grass patches on the coastal greens and next to sheep droppings when higher in the hills.

This was exactly what happened. By counting the characteristic small pits which badgers make to get at the worms, I found that, in the summer up in the hills, 81 per cent were right next to a pile of sheep pellets. On the coastal greens this was only 9 per cent, just as much as could be expected if the badgers dug their pits randomly. There, however, 90 per cent of all worm-pits were in taller grass (which occupied only 39 per cent of the total area). These figures made it look as if the Ardnish badgers had a much easier life than those further east, because their worm supply was so much more predictable: even in dry wether it was still possible to get *L. rubellus*, but *L. terrestris* would have been quite out of reach. However, the actual quantities were small: individual worms in Ardnish weighed only $\frac{1}{15}$ of worms caught on agricultural land, and I calculated that the worm biomass per hectare in Ardnish was only about 8 kg, compared with about 450 kg in New Deer, near the Scottish north-east coast.

There were many other sources of food on Ardnish and the badgers were inclined to use alternatives to earthworms, more than badgers in any other study area. Sheep carcasses were one such source, available at most times of year but especially in spring in the months before lambing. Shepherds treated sheep more or less as if they were wild animals and no one bothered to collect dead ones. These carcasses made a ready source of food for foxes, eagles, ravens, great black-backed gulls, and crows, but I soon learned to recognize sheep carcasses which had been fed on by badgers: no other scavenger made such a mess. Chunks of fleece all over the place, bits eaten from any side, the corpse dragged around, often a badger latrine next to it, there was no way of mistaking what had happened. In contrast, foxes made a clean job, eating the carcass from the loins to start with, with no unnecessary mess at all; they, too, often left droppings. Sheep carcasses were scattered everywhere, but concentrated in the coastal areas.

The rowan tree, another important source of food, was scattered everywhere along the slopes. There were not many of them, but they could produce large quantities of berries, which, from what I saw, were excellent badger fare. Out of curiosity one year I calculated how much was being produced; in Ardnish there were an average 26 rowan trees per square kilometre, with 321 bunches of berries, 54 berries per bunch, and 0.27 grams per berry. This produced 122 kg per km². I estimated that well over half of that falls onto the ground and is eaten by badgers between September and November. Also pignuts grew everywhere, along the slopes, on the coastal flats, in woods, and out in the open; they were usually in lower densities than elsewhere, but they were present in profusion.

The result of all this was that the main, favoured food supply (worms) was thin on the ground and badgers had to work hard for it; it was less concentrated into very rich patches, but more predictable in its presence or absence than the food of badgers in agricultural areas. The alternative foods were used more than elsewhere and were pretty much scattered all along the hills and coasts.

This predictable, but poor, scattered supply of food had an important influence on the badgers' organization in Ardnish: within the confines of a rather large area, they were more or less vagrant. In our other areas we were used to the idea of badgers living in huge setts, some centuries old, large excavations with many entrances, and animals foraging from that central place, returning day after day. For instance, in New Deer I found that badgers (with radio-transmitters) on 87 per cent of the days were in the same sett as they had been on the previous day. In Ardnish, that happened on only 18 per cent of the days: the badgers there were almost always on the move. This could be related to the dispersion of the food. If, as in most of our study areas, food is abundant and it cannot be predicted where it will be found from one day to the next, the best place to stay for a badger will be somewhere in the centre of the area. If, as in Ardnish, the presence of food can be predicted with reasonable probability (or it is everywhere in the range), but there is little of it, then a badger is likely to have diminished food in the place where it foraged the previous night. It would be more efficient then to keep moving about the range, staying in different places, and let the previous day's feeding sites recover. So badgers should use setts scattered throughout their feeding range, rather than a single central one.

One of the effects of this difference in lifestyle was that badger setts on the west coast were only very small, compared with those from the east and south. Ardnish badgers often lived in setts with just a single entrance, or under huge boulders, or between the rocks high on the slopes. We knew dozens of such 'setts', but each was used only infrequently, and when a badger was inside there was often a fresh pile of droppings right in the entrance. This told us that there was an animal inside and presumably also other badgers would know. This sett-marking was quite different from what we saw in other areas where badgers had latrines often close to the sett (but not inside the entrance), or on their range boundary (Chapter 6).

It is, incidentally, this habit of vagrancy and the use of odd single holes or couches under rocks, which brings badgers into conflict with people on the west coast of Scotland. Such places are also used by foxes and shepherds there catch foxes by sending their terriers down likely fox-earths; if the fox is down there, it will be driven out and shot, or the terriers will kill it. However, if there happens to be a badger inside, more often than not the terrier will come off second-best and be seriously injured or killed; many dogs are lost this way. Consequently, many west-coast shepherds will kill badgers whenever they get a chance, however illegal that may be nowadays.

After a year and a half we had to abandon Ardnish as a study area because the land was sold; the sheep were taken off and only red deer now roam the slopes. The change was profound: no more short grass, no more heaps of sheep pellets. When I revisited Ardnish two years later, badgers had all but disappeared, indicating once more that there, too, man with his livestock was more important to badgers than wilderness and solitude.

There was much more that we could have studied in Ardnish, as well as in our other study areas. To me, one of the most important questions which we left unanswered was that of the badgers' foraging 'decisions': when does an animal decide whether to start foraging for worms, or to go to another worm patch, or to find a sheep carcass, or to start digging for pignuts? This is the central question of the badger foraging strategy and we have not addressed it properly. Much more detailed knowledge of the availability of food is needed, but the question is important enough to warrant a special project, and I hope that it will be done soon.

Further details

See Kruuk (1978b, 1986); Kruuk and Parish (1981, 1983, 1985); Kruuk *et al.* (1979). See also Ahnlund (1981); Fowler and Racey (1988); Macdonald (1980b); Mellgren and Roper (1986); Neal (1986); Neal and Harrison (1958); Smith (1974).

6

Territories and numbers in the clans

RANGE SIZE

The extent of the range which a badger uses in an area could possibly be influenced by several different factors and in our project it was clearly of vital importance to determine what exactly those factors were. It was, *a priori*, quite likely that food would play a role, because it does so in many other species of animals. But food could have an effect in many different ways, and there were other, possible environmental influences. Also the number of other badgers could be important. In order to illustrate the way in which the animals use their area, and of how groups of badgers have divided the land between themselves, I will first describe another typical sequence of events during a radio-tracking observation.

Speyside, 10 October 1979, 20.25 hours: I sit on a slope above the Guislich sett, in Speyside. It is cold and windy, and the red deer are roaring somewhere below me. My radio set produces one soft bleep every second; every bleep sounds the same, which means that the radio signal is steady, there is no movement. Male 57 is fast asleep, somewhere down in the sett, under the large oaks at the bottom of the slope. 20.40: First movements detectable in the signal. 20.48: Badger emerges. It is quite dark, the beta-light on the badger glows green, bobbing around the sett entrances. Three minutes later he is off. Down the short slope, along a fence, all in a steady trot. It is easy open terrain, so I can keep up without too much bother; the badger follows the fence between two fields. Thirty metres from the sett he stops, digs and paws the ground. I know that there is a latrine there, and the badger squats, probably defecating, then he is off again.

The steady trot takes the animal across the fields, some 600 metres from the sett, a third of a mile. A bit of scratching here, just nosing around somewhere else: various stops, but what the badger is heading for appears to be a large pasture, just along the edge of some rough woodland, where a herd of Highland cattle has been grazing for the last few weeks. 21.30: It is almost pitch dark, and only my infrared equipment, the hot-eye, can tell me what my quarry is doing now: catching earthworms. I settle down against a large birch tree, watch, record on the dictaphone. One worm is picked up after another, the badger slowly wandering up and down an area of about 50 × 30 metres. It is still cold. 22.10: No change: the badger is worming, but perhaps slowing down a bit. Scanning the field with the hot-eye, I notice three red deer stags a bit lower down, with their heads up; the badger takes no notice. 22.13: Loud roars from one of the stags. It sends shivers down my spine. I don't think that it was the deer which caused the badger to move, but whatever it was, he is off, trotting steadily in a direction at right angles to where he came from.

I walk behind him, as fast as I can. The badger follows a well-defined animal path, which I recognize as a badger path, up a small hill, down the other side, straight towards a curiously shaped juniper bush. He stops, scratches the grass vigorously, sending clumps of earth around. He makes a quick, squatting movement, then he leaves, and trots up a slope again between the birch trees. 22.40: The animal reaches another pasture, a rough one this time. He stops, then starts worming. A slightly larger patch, but the same pattern: worm after worm. I have to stay absolutely still in one spot, watching continuously, whilst he moves back and forth in front of me. Almost an hour he is at it, and I feel absolutely freezing cold. 23.45: We are off again, but this time I have a mishap: the badger makes a sharp turn just in front of me and catches my scent. He does not pause to savour the experience: a sudden rush, and off he goes at full speed, and there is no way in which I can keep up with that. I head back for the bothy, for a quick cup of coffee, and a bit of heat. It is not until almost two hours later that I again find no. 57, about a kilometre from where he gave me the slip.

This observation was a fairly typical sequence of events; most radio-tracking of badgers consisted of variations on such a theme. There would be a fairly fast movement over an area where little food was found, then long periods of intensive foraging in a small area. In between, badgers might visit latrines and follow badger paths, both of which I had learned to recognize as territorial boundary features. In summer, in really dry periods, badgers could wander around their area without spending any length of time in particular places, without patch-feeding, but that was the exception rather than the rule.

Over the years we collected numerous records such as the one I have just mentioned, in several of our study areas. Later, we began to speed things up, collecting data on up to 20 badgers more or less simultaneously by driving around in the Land Rover at night, picking up a signal, recognizing the animal from the radio-frequency, locating the badger with a few fixes and spotting the beta-light, then moving on again to the next badger. The disadvantage of such methods was that we only got information about the animals' size of range and movements within the range boundaries, but nothing on the actual behaviour of the animals, which after all was the most interesting part of our project. Without the detailed observations on patch-feeding, we would never have understood what determines the size of the badgers' ranges.

Slowly a picture began to build up of who went where and exactly how the boundaries lay between the badgers from neighbouring setts. Badgers are very frustrating animals for studying these problems, simply because of their patch-feeding habit; on any particular night they use only a small part of their range and observations are needed over many nights to build up a complete map. Fortunately, we still had another string to our bow, i.e. coloured bait-marking, the method I had first used in Wytham.

Basically, this method uses the badgers' habit of defecating on the often conspicuous latrines, usually located on the range boundaries. We gave badgers something conspicuous to eat which they could not digest and it would turn up in those latrines. What we did, in fact, was to put some small pieces of red plastic, mixed with a spoonful of peanuts and treacle, next to an entrance of a sett. Then we did the same with bits of blue plastic on a sett a kilometre further along the slope. We would find latrines with scats with bits of red, and other scats with bits of blue, somewhere between the two setts on the clan range boundary. We obtained great satisfaction in drawing coloured lines on a map, connecting the main setts (Fig. 6.1) with yet more different latrines, which were also marked as dots (Fig. 6.2). In the field it looked like a map with the coloured fronts of warring parties, fronts which we advanced with increasing knowledge of the situation.

It took three years with these different methods before we had a reasonably accurate idea of how large the ranges were in the various study areas. There were large differences and in general badgers used larger areas here than further south in England. Typically, in our main study area in

FIG. 6.1. The main sett, centre of activity of the territory. Adult male and four-months-old cub, just after emerging in the early evening. (Photograph by R. Tanner.)

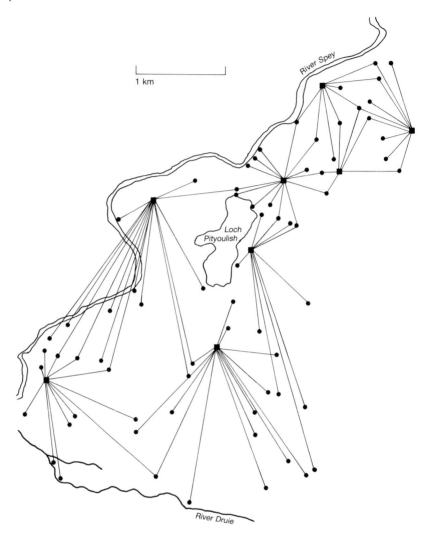

FIG. 6.2. Observations of colour markers which were fed to badgers on main setts (black squares) and were found again in latrines (small dots), Speyside, 1981.

Speyside, each range was between 100 and 300 hectares (250–750 acres, about 0.5–1.0 square mile) and in Ardnish and the agricultural richness of New Deer between 150 and 200 hectares. The smallest range I had found near Oxford was 21 hectares, although the more usual size was 50 hectares. These are the ranges, or territories, of whole groups or clans of badgers, animals all living more or less together in one main sett. I will say more about this later, but individual badgers may have ranges that are somewhat smaller than the total clan territory and there is the odd one which uses the ranges of several clans.

As in the earlier observation, when we were walking behind our radio-badgers at night, we were very much aware of the fact that we often spent hours in one place, then quickly covered a long stretch or a steep hillside, panting, until our target decided to stay a long time in one spot again. In other words, there was a lot of unused ground between the places badgers used for feeding. Heather, and usually also arable land (except when barley was ripe), was used almost only as a thoroughfare, but the animals spent many hours in relatively small parts of grassland and woods. The patchy nature of these badger ranges shows clearly in pictures of the landscape.

In every badger range the animals used several feeding areas, not just one. The reason for this was probably the fact that, although very rich, each of the feeding sites had periods when no food was available to badgers: the grass might be too long when cattle were grazed elsewhere, or the wind from a particular direction might force worms underground, or there might be no dew in that one site (consequently no worms) and a heavy dew elsewhere.

I reasoned that if these feeding areas or 'patches' (Fig. 6.3), i.e. parts of pastures, suitable woods, etc., were indeed a consistent feature of the badger territory, then the distances between pastures, and between them and the

FIG. 6.3. A 'feeding patch' for badgers in Speyside, grazed short by Highland cattle.

worm-rich woodlands, should be important in deciding how large an area a badger needs. The question was how that idea could be tested.

Considering different study areas, it seemed that a badger had to walk further to get to a good feeding site in Speyside, compared to an animal living in Wytham. To quantify this, I put some random points on the map and measured the distance from them to the five nearest possible feeding sites for badgers (pastures and broad-leaved woods). I took the average of five, because that was about the number of feeding patches badgers used in their ranges, but it turned out that that number is not important, as I obtained similar results when I used the average of 10 patch distances. I called this figure the *food-patch distance*. The potential feeding sites I considered were, of course, all the pastures and broad-leaved woodlands, not just those in which I had actually seen badgers. In this way, for each area I found a *mean food-patch distance*, a figure which characterized the *distribution* of feedings sites, not the quality or their size.

To compare that figure with some distance measure which characterized the size of badger ranges, I took simply the average distance between the badger's main setts. The reason was that it was easy to measure, especially in areas where we did not know the exact boundaries of the territories, and I was keen to use it for areas other than our own study sites. It was easy to show that the distance between neighbouring setts was closely correlated with the size of territories, as calculated from our radio-tracking and colour-marking experiments (Fig. 6.4).

We therefore knew the mean food-patch distance and also the badgers' neighbour distance, and when we compared them they were very neatly correlated (Fig. 6.5), which meant that in an area where pastures were far apart the badger setts were also far apart, and animals lived in larger ranges. If instead of using the distance between food patches and random points we used the distance between those patches and the main setts, we obtained a similar result (Fig. 6.6).

Although I was only able to show that there existed a correlation between the size of the ranges of badger clans and the dispersion of their main food resource, it is tempting to conclude that this food dispersion actually causes the badger ranges to be smaller or larger. There are a few problems with this. First, it was theoretically possible that something else was correlated with both food dispersion and badger range size, which might be what the badger range size was responding to. This could be food biomass for instance; however, we were in fact able to show that food biomass is not related to range size (see below). Second, the ranges of individual badgers tended to be smaller than that of the whole clan, sometimes less than one-half of it. The significance of this became somewhat clearer when we looked at it over a longer period, and I will discuss this in Chapter 8.

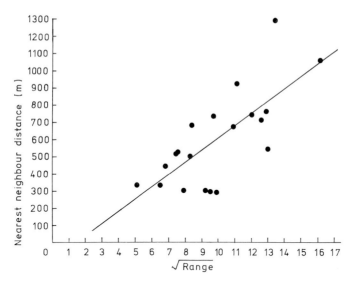

FIG. 6.4. The relation between the range size of badgers (in hectares) and the distance from the main sett to the nearest neighbouring main sett (in metres) ($r=0.73, p<0.001$) (from Kruuk and Parish 1982).

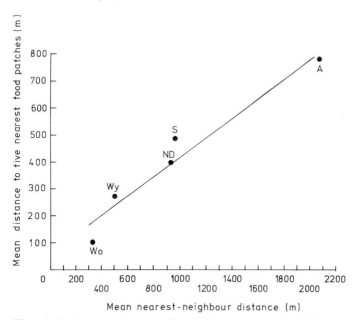

FIG. 6.5. The relation between the mean distance between nearest-neighbour setts in an area and the mean distance to the five nearest potential food patches from random points ($r=0.97, p<0.01$). A=Ardnish, S=Speyside, ND=New Deer, Wy=Wytham, Wo=Woodchester Park (Cotswolds, courtesy Dr C. Cheeseman) (from Kruuk and Parish 1982).

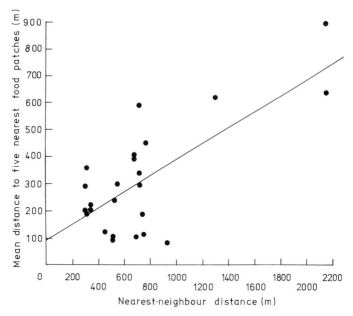

FIG. 6.6. The relation between the distance from a main sett to its nearest neighbour and the mean distance from that main sett to the five nearest food patches ($r=0.74$, $p<0.001$). Data from all Scottish areas and Wytham (from Kruuk and Parish 1982).

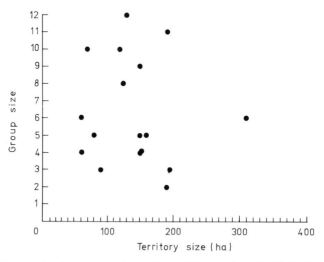

FIG. 6.7. The relation between territory size and the number of adult badgers per clan ($r=-0.07$, not significant) (from Kruuk and Parish 1982).

DEFENCE OF THE TERRITORY

In the somewhat complicated explanation of the size of the area occupied by badgers, I find myself sometimes using the word *range* (or *home range*), sometimes *territory*. Care must be taken because the two terms are not the same, and there is a great deal of literature on the correct terminology. Luckily, for badgers it appears to be all the same thing: the range, or home range, is a defended area, a proper *territory* in the accepted sense of the word.

I have seen several fights between badgers, but the one in which the animals best demonstrated the point I made in the previous paragraph occurred in Oxfordshire, not in Scotland. The following is an account of that observation, from a paper in the *Journal of Zoology*.

On 25 August 1974, at 01.50 hours, male no. 7, a large radio-collared male from the Jew's Harp clan, was walking on the boundary path between his clan range and that of the neighbouring Brogden's clan, in open pasture land. He passed a slightly smaller badger of the Brogden's clan, which was foraging about 50 m from the boundary on his own side. Both appeared to notice each other (heads up briefly), but continued with their previous activities. About 100 m further, male no. 7 left the boundary path and walked slowly, whilst feeding on worms, into the field which was inside the Brogden's range. In doing so, he moved upwind of the Brogden's badger, and when male no. 7 had been foraging for 12 minutes in his neighbour's range, this other badger suddenly ran up to him. Male no. 7 ran back to his own range, but was overtaken after a few metres and bitten in the rump. He escaped and ran across the boundary, pursued by his neighbour for about 30 m inside his own area. Then he suddenly turned and the other badger ran back, chased by male no. 7 about 50 m inside the Brogden's range. The neighbour turned back and chased male no. 7 back into the Jew's Harp range. During this last chase, the two badgers almost ran into me on the boundary; both took fright and ran off to their respective setts. During this interaction no sound was uttered except for soft 'keckering' growls at the turning point of the zigzag, and at the point of physical contact.

This description does not do justice to the excitement of such an event; to be surrounded by two furious badgers, in the darkness of a summer night in the English countryside, with something very significant happening right there, where only I could see it—I can still remember every detail. Apart from the fight itself, the observation involved many other details of badger territoriality: the special paths exactly on the border, the latrines with their violent scrape-marks. For badgers, these were places which were obviously highly important and they spent a great deal of time on their boundaries.

For the human visitor, the border paths and latrines are the most conspicuous manifestation of badgers' territoriality; the actual fights mostly happen at times when the animals cannot be seen. Those fights can be vicious, with the contestants inflicting horrible wounds on each other as illustrated by this field observation in Speyside, about 10 o'clock one night in March 1979.

I am radio-tracking a young male in the Loch clan area, an animal which we had nicknamed Hitler (he behaved unusually aggressively towards us whenever he got himself into a trap, and he had only one testicle). After I have been with him for almost an hour, he crosses into the neighbours' territory, the Sheilich range, which I know as the area where he had been born and where he grew up, his native clan. After twenty minutes, still within two hundred metres from the border, he is suddenly confronted by an animal which I also recognize as one with a nickname: Cauliflower (because of his crumpled ears). He is the very old resident boar of the Sheilich clan, and presumably his father. I cannot see the exact sequence of events, because it all happens inside a large juniper bush; but the upshot of it is a ball of growling fury, keckering noises, for only about twenty seconds, then Hitler is off, back in the direction of the Loch again, bleeding from a wound on his rump. (Two weeks later, when I had him in a trap again, I noticed deep bite wounds on his lower back, just above the tail, with a large patch of skin torn off. However, whether his old father inflicted this on him, or some other badger, was of course impossible to say.)

Both these fights happened to be between males, but the sows were also intolerant of intruders. Whether they were equal to the boars in their territoriality was impossible to say, because we did not get enough observations of fights. But we did notice that in those, regrettably few, fights where we knew the sex of both badgers, male attacked male, female attacked female. I think that this was tied up with the relations between the sexes within the clan.

After seeing the fights and boundary markings, I have no doubt that badgers are intensely territorial animals, more so than most other carnivores, and highly aggressive towards their neighbours, spending a lot of time and energy in the defence of their own area. I still find this very puzzling; why should these animals bother so much with aggression over exact boundaries? Would it not be much more efficient if the animals would just forage in an area around the sett, and if one badger should eat some of the worms in the neighbouring home range then the neighbour can do the same in return? Since the size of their ranges appears to be related to the distribution of food, I am assuming that badgers defend their food resources against their neighbours' greed. But in that case, why should male attack only male and sows only other sows? This suggests sexual competition, rather than fights over food. The time of year when these fights happen does not tell us much; probably most fighting occurs in spring, but aggression has

PLATE 1. Large male badger in the aggressive 'Upright' posture.

PLATE 2. Part of a clan near the entrance of the sett.

PLATE 3. Wytham Woods, near Oxford.

PLATE 4. Pityoulish and Rothiemurchus, Speyside.

Plate 5. Glen Feshie.

Plate 6. Ardnish on the west coast.

PLATE 7. Monymusk area on the east coast.

PLATE 8. New Deer on the east coast.

PLATE 9. Badger female with radio-collar; 'earthworming' in pasture.

PLATE 10. *Lumbricus terrestris* foraging on the surface at night. Note tail end in burrow.

PLATE 11. Lamb killed by badger, with characteristic injuries.

PLATE 12. Adult male badger eating a rabbit, with female in foreground.

PLATE 15. Male (foreground) and female badger near sett entrance.

PLATE 16. Large badger sett above Loch Pityoulish in Speyside. Six of the 12 entrances are visible.

PLATE 17. Latrine near a field fence.

PLATE 18. Badger sow dragging bedding back to her sett, going backwards.

PLATE 19. Badger mother (right) taking food back to her cub.

PLATE 20. Recently killed badger club (about 4 weeks old) outside sett.

PLATE 21. Anal region of an immobilized badger male, showing the large opening of the sub-caudal gland with the white secretion, located above the anus. The brown colour is due to secretions of the anal glands.

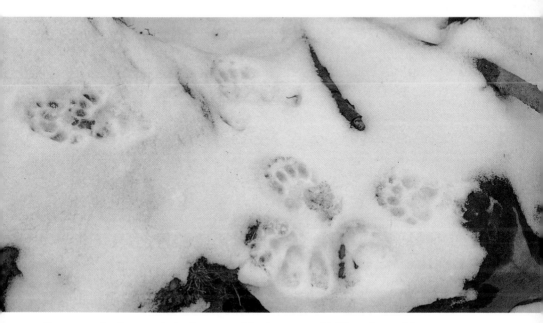

PLATE 22. Badger tracks in the snow with a 'squat-mark'. The colour of the squat-mark indicates its origin in sub-caudal and anal glands.

PLATE 23. Badger boar squat-marking.

been seen at most times of year. Most matings happen in the spring, but also food intake is highest then.

The problem of why badgers are so very territorial was especially highlighted once I started to study otters, animals which belong to the same family of Mustelids as badgers but which hardly seem to bother about defence. Why should one species do it and another not? Obviously, at this stage we still do not know enough about badgers to give a plausible answer. One possibility is that the explanation is complex, concerning both sex and food reasons. Perhaps badgers defend their territory so fiercely because what is paramount to them is not so much the resources themselves, as *their own knowledge of those resources*, their experience with what is available where and when. For a badger it could be important that no other strange badger comes in and upsets this; on the other hand, if that strange badger happens to be one of the opposite sex, the advantages of its presence may outweigh the disadvantages.

Such an 'explanation' assumes that for different species this knowledge of where food can be found is of different importance. An alternative explanation would be that it is the patchiness of the food distribution within the territory which calls for a much more vigorous defence than a more homogenous dispersion: some patches could be vital during a particular time of year. Once a badger loses a patch to the neighbours, this may endanger the integrity of the whole territory. One way of testing such different hypotheses would be to compare various carnivores, intra- as well as inter-specifically, once we know more about patterns of food availability in several species, which would be quite a task, even in the better known animals.

DEMARCATION OF BORDERS

The boundaries of the badgers' ranges were not only defended with direct aggression, they were also frequently clearly marked with signs visible to us, though badgers probably just smelled them. These were paths, latrines, and tussocks used for 'squat-marking'. All this was especially conspicuous in high-density areas or where there was a boundary close to the main sett. In fact, these signs were also found close to setts and far from boundaries, but in the field the association with boundaries was quite unambiguous.

Paths especially were often associated with setts, but they also occurred exactly on the border between ranges (Fig. 6.8). They were used by badgers, and presumably they were also made by them, and were often very conspicuous in areas where the border crossed large tracts of land such as open woodlands or fields, without the landmarks of fences, or roads, usually associated with boundaries.

FIG. 6.8. Badger path made and almost exclusively used by badgers, demarcating the exact borderline between two clan territories.

I will say more about squat-marking in Chapter 9, because it is an important and very interesting means of communication. It was done particularly often on the boundary paths, by males as well as by females: it was clearly associated with territorial behaviour. But the most conspicuous indicators of the badger border were the latrines which were aggregations of up to 60 defecations, in small pits dug by the badgers themselves. Each pit was 5 to 10 cm deep, though sometimes as much as 30 cm, and contained one or several droppings, or often nothing. There were often signs of vigorous scratching of the ground around the latrine. Latrines were used at all times of the year, but especially in spring (February to April) with a second, lower peak in October. Many latrines were used by badgers for several years; some of the first latrines I found in Wytham as a student in 1963 are still being used now, in 1988. The droppings were not covered. Often some yellow, brownish jelly-like substance was found in the pits; I used to think that it was a secretion of the anal glands, but having compared the secretions I now know that to be wrong. It must originate somewhere deep in the intestine and may well be merely a defecation without food remains.

When a badger visited a latrine it spent 20 to 90 seconds performing several different behaviour patterns such as squat-marking (pressing the anal region on vegetation or hummocks), vigorous scratching with forelegs and hindlegs, digging of pits, defecation and urination in a pit. Probably all these activities involved the deposition of various glandular secretions, from anal, sub-caudal, inter-digital and other glands. Most latrines were on the territorial boundary and those that were more inside the territory were smaller (on the border a latrine had an average 14 droppings, but only 8 elsewhere). Also very striking was the position of the latrines close to some conspicuous land mark (Table 6.1), a fence, a track, or a woodland edge, much more often than would be expected if badgers had made them somewhere randomly. Because of that they were quite easy to find once we knew where to look. The landmarks reinforced the striking pattern of territorial boundaries, of home ranges which are defended by all possible means, and with a large input of energy, against the neighbours.

NUMBERS OF BADGERS PER TERRITORY

The question of how many badgers live together in one sett was very relevant to one of the main reasons why I started to study badgers in the first place: to discover the biological function of their gregariousness. It also follows on closely after the previous discussion of home range size and territory. First, therefore, I will describe the number of badgers in each clan

TABLE 6.1. Landmarks near badger latrines. Landmarks were recorded when within 10 m of a latrine, but usually they were less than 3 m distance. Some latrines were located near several kinds of landmark, therefore percentages do not add up to 100. Number of latrines in sample = 111; difference between observed and random: $\chi^2 = 28.1$, degrees of freedom = 5, $p < 0.001$. Data from Wytham Woods (Kruuk 1978a).

Type of landmark	Observed latrines (%)	Expected if latrines randomly distributed (%)
Car track	40	11
Vegetation boundary (e.g. woodland edge)	34	14
Fence (usually barbed wire)	31	15
Single conifer tree	9	0
Others (pylon; single tree in field)	2	2
None	31	69

and how we set about estimating them, before going into detail of how the clans are structured and the relations between the members.

Perhaps the best way of conveying the difficulty of estimating badger numbers in a clan is through a description of a field observation.

June 1978. Darkness approaches in a huge, old plantation of very large spruce trees, in New Deer, close to the north-east point of Scotland. I sit on a wobbly little platform against a tree, above a large badger sett, rain dripping down my neck, the woods dead silent. There are midges, too, but fortunately I have managed to keep them more or less at bay, by chemical means. Close to the sett are the remains of a large, stone-age chambered cairn, hence the name Cairn clan. The badgers here have given me quite a lot of difficulties. Their sett is enormous, twenty-three entrances, with big spoil heaps everywhere, over an area of about a quarter of a hectare (half an acre); apart from this main sett, there are well-used outlying holes in the woods nearby. Obviously, there are quite a lot of animals here, and I have no idea how many: there may be five, ten, twenty or more. It is vital to find out, but it seems a hopeless situation, overwhelmingly difficult.

Tonight I am not faring any better than usual. Forty minutes after I settled on my platform, a large boar shows his face in one of the nearest holes. A bit later he is out, sitting in front of his exit, noisily scratching his belly. Only minutes later two more badgers are out, either sows or younger males, difficult to recognize (incidentally, I often have the impression that that belly scratching of the male acts as a signal for other badgers). These other animals don't stay around, disappearing onto the other part of the sett, where many dead branches obscure my view, I think I hear them leaving, crashing around in the wood, but I can never be certain; perhaps they went down another hole in the far part of the set. Within 10 minutes, there are badger noises coming from everywhere, shapes walking below me, into holes, out of other ones, and there is no way of recognizing them. Soon, all goes quiet again, leaving me dripping on my platform, nowhere nearer a solution of that question of numbers.

For this kind of situation the 'labelling' of badgers with zinc-65 (Chapter 3) proved to be a good solution and it enabled us, after many attempts at other methods, to come up with reliable estimates. In the spruce woods near New Deer, with their huge badger setts, we collected many hundreds of droppings over several months. It appeared that it was not very surprising that I had not been able to count the badgers there, just by sitting above their holes: the Cairn clan numbered 11 adult badgers, as well as several cubs. The clan next to this one was not quite so populous, numbering eight members; even so, it had been quite impossible to establish that by just using the hot-eye or binoculars, pencil, and paper.

Over the years we managed to obtain estimates of badger clans in all our study areas. In fact, in Speyside we continued doing this for a long time, to see how numbers changed over the years, with fascinating results; I will come back to this later. Wherever we could, we compared our estimates with what we thought were present, based on either direct observations or sometimes just intuition; we were never far out. This cross-checking was important, because we found it quite difficult to explain the results, especially in the beginning.

What we could not understand, at first, was that there appeared to be no relation at all between the size of a clan's territory and the number of badgers in it. Somehow we expected to find that a small range would contain only few animals and a large range many. What we found (Fig. 6.7, p. 82) showed in fact that range size and clan size were quite independent of each other, which meant that these two variables were controlled, or limited, in entirely different ways. A clan, at least in any of our study areas, could contain anywhere between one and twelve adult badgers; usually there were between three and six (average 5.4). A clan of six badgers could live in an area of 60 hectares, another of exactly the same number of animals could occupy 300 hectares. Conversely, one territory of almost 200 hectares housed two badgers, while another territory of the same size elsewhere was used by eleven animals. These group sizes are by no means extremes for the badger; in southern England especially they go up to twenty or more, and recently urban badger clans (which were being fed by people) in England were found with thirty members.

Having found earlier that territories were larger in places where feeding areas were far apart, or, more exactly, that territory size and food dispersion were correlated, we therefore had to look for a quite different factor in the badgers' environment which could possible influence the numbers of animals in a clan, the group size. It seemed logical to test whether perhaps food biomass or productivity played a role here.

Fortunately, we knew quite a lot about food, especially worm densities in different areas. As I described in Chapter 4 we had looked at the availability of the badgers' main foods and since earthworms were by far the most important prey I concentrated the argument on them. Collecting data on numbers of *Lumbricus* had been tedious, involving hours and hours of waiting for worms to come to the surface of a patch of grass after we had poured formalin on it. It was worth while, however, and relating worm numbers to badger numbers produced some fascinating results.

The first inkling we had that numbers of individuals in the clan were affected by food resources came when we found that so many badgers were living together in setts like the one I described above, in that green, rich farmland in the New Deer area, known as one of the best farming areas in Scotland. It made sense then to calculate what badgers actually had available to them, within their territory. On average, 10.5 *Lumbricus* crawled to the surface in a randomly chosen square metre there, which amounted to 105 000 kg in just one badger territory. At the other extreme, in Ardnish on the west coast, we obtained only 1200 kg of worms from a badger range—still a great many worms, but two orders of magnitude smaller than in the east. These were extremes, to give an idea of the kind of differences that were involved. There was a direct relationship between numbers of worms and numbers of badgers in a badger territory (Fig. 6.9).

This meant that we could relate the size of the badgers' territory to the way in which worms were distributed, and the numbers of animals inhabiting the territory to the worm density (presumably, what was important was not so much worm density as worm productivity, but that was more difficult to measure). Taken together, territory size and group size are the two measures of overall *population density*, at least with animals such as badgers, where there is little overlap between neighbouring ranges. We could also look at the relation between this overall population density and worm density; it was not surprising then that that, too, appeared to be a simple positive correlation (Fig. 6.10). In none of our Scottish study areas did we have a really high badger density; it varied between about 1 and 8 per square kilometre (2.5–20 per square mile) between the west and east coast of Scotland, with our Speyside study area in the middle with 2.2 per km². These densities are fairly normal when compared with figures from Sweden, Holland, France, and other countries, but they are low in comparison with the figures from Chris Cheeseman's study area in the Cotswolds, in the south of England: he found about 20 badgers per square kilometre (50 per square mile).

CHANGES IN THE SIZE OF RANGES AND GROUPS

In countries where badgers are not dependent upon earthworms, the arrangement of territories and groups must be organized differently, and I

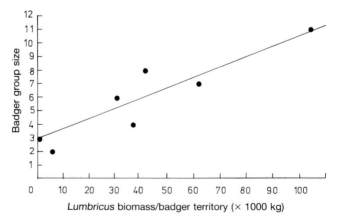

FIG. 6.9. The relation between *Lumbricus* biomass per territory and the number of badgers in the clan ($r = 0.91$, $p < 0.01$) (from Kruuk and Parish 1982).

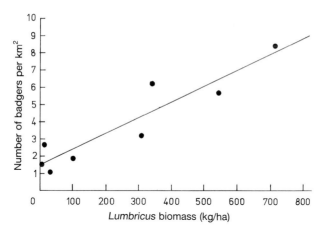

FIG. 6.10. The relation between *Lumbricus* biomass and the overall density of badgers in the Scottish study areas ($r = 0.93$, $p < 0.001$) (from Kruuk and Parish 1982).

think we have as yet little idea how. It would be fascinating, for instance, to look at this in the mountains of northern Italy, where Lil de Kock and I found that badgers ate mostly olives and other fruit, throughout the year, with olives and other fruits almost assuming the role of earthworms in north-west Europe, and badger feeding areas moving annually up and down the mountain slopes—low in winter, high in summer. There remains a lot more work to be done there and in other countries on the different resources for badgers.

In the meantime, after a few years of our study we came to recognize that in Scotland also the badger spatial organization could be more complicated than the picture I painted here. Basically, what we had done so far was to look at badgers and food across a spectrum of landscapes, comparing differences, producing a static picture. This certainly helped us to understand the animals, but a social system is not static. In order to look for possible complications, to see what happened if one studied these relations between badger and food over long periods, we concentrated for several years on our study area in Scotland's centre, Speyside. The questions we asked in the five-year study there were essentially similar to what we had done across the map of Scotland before: what happens to clans from year to year; what happens to boundaries; and what happens to food supplies? In finding the answers to those questions, we spent hundreds of nights radio-tracking; it would have been impossible to do this without the help of several dedicated and enthusiastic students. The answers confirmed much of what we had already found, but they also showed complications caused, probably, by some rather drastic changes in local agriculture.

On the farm which was our most important study area in Speyside, various things had happened, including a change in management. Most important, during the time we worked there a substantial drop in the numbers of earthworms had occurred. Changes in farming practice were the likely cause, the *Lumbricus* numbers fell considerably over five years (from 12.2 to 2.7 per m² in one half of the area and from 7.1 to 5.8 per m² in the other). Pasture distribution changed little; the mean distance from random points to five nearest pastures fluctuated around 436 m, with a standard error of only 8 m over the years. So we expected to find no change in territory boundaries, but we did predict a drop in badger numbers, in the size of the clans there. It was an interesting opportunity to test some of our ideas and it showed that although our predictions largely came true, the relationships were not quite as simple as we had thought.

One of the most obvious general findings was that the average size of the ranges of the badger clans did not change significantly: it fluctuated, but there was no overall increase or decrease over the years. The mean range size stayed between 176 and 236 hectares and differences between years were not significant, largely because the average for each year was made up of such hugely differing range sizes (for instance, in 1980 the smallest clan range was 24 hectares, the largest 324), and with only eight badger territories to work on the fluctuations of the average then do not mean much.

Badger numbers per clan declined over the five years, from 5.3 to 3.6, but despite the fact that this was a 32 per cent decrease this trend was not statistically significant because of the small numbers of clans we could work with. I had expected badger numbers to fall, so this result was in the right direction, but inconclusive. Perhaps we could have expected an even larger decrease; I think that the main reason between the expected and observed difference was that I had oversimplified the badgers' ecology when I only considered earthworms in this relationship; when earthworm numbers fell, badgers started to eat much more barley.

Taking badger food over the whole year, the animals' diet in 1976 consisted of over 60 per cent (by volume) of earthworms and less than 10 per cent of cereals; in 1982 less than 40 per cent was earthworms and over 20 per cent barley. Clearly badgers did not make this change easily and their individual weights dropped by almost 15 per cent (Chapter 5). In other words, badgers responded to the change in conditions by changing their diet, and although they did not do well out of this, they did sustain their numbers better than expected. I do not think that we fully understand this. It seemed simple to find that if a preferred food disappears, animals switch to a less preferred one; but the question remains why badgers did not take more of the alternatives in the first place, if food is, indeed, a limiting factor.

After our study had finished, badgers numbers did go down further. Paul Latour, whose PhD study was on 'our' Speyside badgers, found fewer animals, especially in the range where earthworm numbers had suffered most. Also, in the years that he studied there, he found no evidence of badgers breeding in the two clans on which he concentrated.

We noticed other changes in the life of the badgers, changes I had not predicted. Most noticeably, although the clan territory size had not shown any overall trend over the years, the area of the group territory which was used by each individual badger increased quite substantially (Fig. 6.11). This implied that with decreasing worm numbers individual badgers used the communal territory more extensively than they did initially. In the beginning an average animal, whether male or female, used about 45 per cent of the clan range in any particular year. This figure steadily climbed to 75 per cent in our last year there, so again indicating that the badgers were

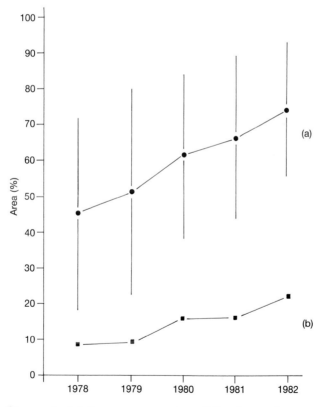

FIG. 6.11. Changes in (a) the mean percentage of the clan territory used by each individual badger, and (b) the percentage of overlap between neighbouring ranges (i.e. area used by more than one clan) (from Kruuk and Parish 1987).

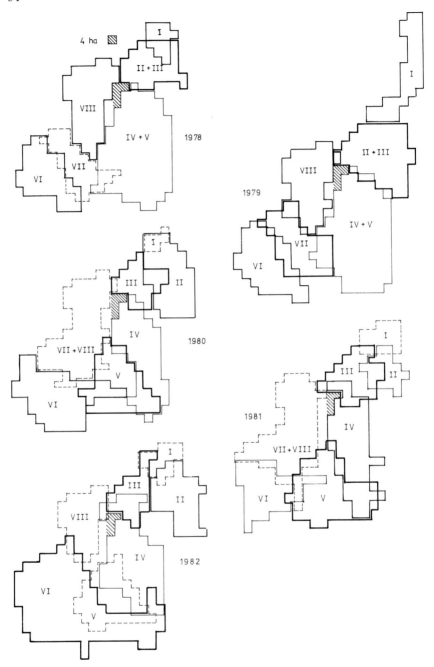

FIG. 6.12. Computerized map of the territories of clans in Speyside and the changes from 1978 to 1982. The central loch is indicated by the hatched area (from Kruuk and Parish 1987).

harder pressed than before, or at least that they changed their foraging efforts and somehow managed to get enough food without changing the fabric of the spatial organization too much. But there was also evidence that their social life was affected by all this; they became more solitary. I will return to this in Chapter 8.

Finally, we noted an increase in the overlap of neighbouring ranges. In the beginning of the study no more than 9 per cent of the total area was used by more than one clan, but this figure increased to 23 per cent five years later (Fig. 6.11). This increase in overlap is shown in the computerized maps of Fig. 6.12. What these maps also show is the large year-to-year variation in boundary configurations, despite the fact that the overall territory size changed little. This, too, was something I had not foreseen; I had expected the territories to remain unaltered.

To end this chapter I want to return to the effects of earthworms, or rather to the effects of food in general, on territory size and clan size. At the risk of belabouring the point, I think the previous pages show how important it is in animals such as badgers to think in terms of *range size* and *group size* and not just about that one, single figure called *population density*. It makes sense to relate population-limiting mechanisms to groups, not just to overall density, and it makes sense to relate the susceptibility to disease (e.g. bovine tuberculosis) to the size of population units in which these animals occur. Patterns of dispersion, of food as well as of the animals themselves, are at least as important as simple, all-embracing figures of density.

Further details

See Kruuk (1978*a,b*, 1986); Kruuk and Parish (1982, 1987). See also Cheeseman *et al.* (1981, 1987, 1988); Harris (1982); Latour (1988).

7

Badgers in captivity

HISTORY OF THE CAPTIVE CLAN

At the beginning of the study it was clear that the problem of finding out what happens *within* the clan, of describing the social behaviour and organization of the members, would be very difficult. Even with our excellent night vision equipment, radio-transmitters, and other techniques we still often missed what happened in the undergrowth; we could only focus on particular animals whilst many other interactions might be taking place out of sight. And even if we could observe behaviour patterns and relationships, even if we did know the identity of the animals we were looking at, it was still difficult to know the individual history of the animals involved.

This problem was not just an academic one. If, indeed, the numbers of badgers within a clan were limited by the amount of food to be found in its range, there should be some behavioural mechanism that would organize this. Perhaps a dominance order, or a straight scramble competition, maybe just a first-come-first-served system, maybe a system of birth control, a limitation of numbers based on mortality, or on emigration. There were many possibilities, and we were interested because it was an essential part of the main question. It was also important to find out more about the social organization if ever badger populations were to be managed, to control numbers because of problems with bovine TB, to move badgers to other areas, and so on.

We argued that to breed our own clan could provide at least some help. Of course, what happens in captivity cannot be extrapolated directly to what goes on in the wild, but depending on the conditions in which captive animals are kept, they can give indications of what to look for in the wild, and not just in their social relationships but also when foraging. Conversely, capital animals can provide possible explanations for observations on wild badgers. Tame animals can be used for behavioural experiments, even in the species' natural habitat. Extreme care must be taken with this, but with due consideration captive animals can provide unique information.

Captive animals also give unexpected insights into the way a species moves through its landscape. This is something difficult to rationalize, but somehow the handling and observing of an animal at very close range enables one to get an almost instinctive idea about how the animal reacts and behaves in the wild. It is hard to quantify or to describe usefully in a publication, but it is an experience that helps greatly when following animals in the field. Lastly, it is also tremendously enjoyable really to know individual animals that are not afraid.

For all these reasons we decided to create a clan territory in the woods next to the Institute of Terrestrial Ecology, in Banchory. We wanted to stock it with badgers whose individual history we knew, watch their every move, and describe the social structure which developed. Here I want to describe the main history of that captive clan.

In the birch woods around our Institute, well away from any other human inhabitation, we had a small one-room building with a deep cellar underneath it, originally an air-raid shelter. Inside we built large brick boxes, with wooden lids and observation windows; in the cellar we made a group of glass-fronted chambers along one wall, connected with each other and the outside world by badger-sized tunnels. Next to the badger house we built an enclosure, up and over a small hill (Fig. 7.1). It was only a quarter

Fig. 7.1. Captive badgers on the scales in their enclosure at night. The seasonal fluctuations in the weight of the animals could be measured without interfering with them.

of a hectare in size, but because of the dense birch and broom, and because of the slope, it appeared to be much larger.

I wanted to emulate a natural clan of four or more animals, but at the time I did not know what a clan really consisted of. In the wild several animals of both sexes were involved, but how were they related to each other? After discussions and advice from many quarters, it was decided to put a number of adult, unrelated badgers together and let them sort themselves out—with careful supervision, of course, in case of trouble.

Tim arrived as a small cub, within a few months of the start of our project, sent to us by a wildlife park in Bristol. I bottle-reared him at home, then installed him at the Institute when he became too boisterous, taking him for long walks on the area on a lead (Fig. 7.2). He was a beautiful animal, but by the time he was half-a-year old quite unmanageable. In the late autumn of 1975, still in his first year of life, he weighed 12 kg, as much as any wild male several years old. He was confident, very active, and highly aggressive towards people, especially to me.

The next animal to arrive in the enclosure was an old female, Fatty, left to

FIG. 7.2. Taking an adolescent male for a walk to study feeding behaviour and scent marking.

us by the disbanding Aberdeen Zoo. She moved in without any problems, the two largely ignored each other and slept together in daytime, and there was no trouble. But later in that first winter trouble did come. That was when a group of five other badgers arrived, all adults, all reared from wild cubs by the same wildlife park in Bristol. All five were between three and six years old: two males (Rumpy and Jack) and three females (Vicky, Small, and One-Lug). Small and One-Lug were sisters, but the rest were unrelated and unknown to each other. They arrived in one box and in our ignorance we put them all together in the large enclosure, assuming that the animals had masses of space and places to get out of each others' way, if need be.

After a couple of days aggression started, with fights, chases, loud growls, and keckering noises. There were days when things went well and we believed we had made it; days when the badgers each went their own way and we thought we had the start of a clan as it was in the wild; but once again there would be a high-intensity fight, driving me to despair. We had to interfere on numerous occasions and in the end several of the badgers had to be housed separately, in smaller pens, and nursed back to health after being severely mauled by others. There is no doubt that if I had not rescued the defeated badgers they would have been killed.

One month after the inauspicious start of the captive group, young Tim was the only male left, having fought off the other, older ones, each of which were put in their own small enclosure. Other outcasts were our first female, Fatty, who was constantly set upon by all the other sows, and Vicky, severely injured by One-Lug, who was now clearly the dominant female in the group. Fatty and Rump shared a small pen without problems and so did Vicky and Jack.

The injuries of the badgers, after their fights, were very characteristic. Invariably, they had a large wound immediately above the root of the tail, sometimes a deep one with a large part of skin removed. There were also frequently wounds in the side of the neck, just behind the head. These injury patterns are also often observed in wild badgers, especially in the high-density areas in southern England. The badgers recover fast; their powers of recuperation are much greater than ours. But there was no doubt that for them to survive I had to separate them from each other when things had gone too far; if I had left them they would have been killed. The losers in fights would lie totally dejected somewhere in a corner of the enclosure and I could often handle them without any extra precautions. After all this aggression I find it difficult to accept badgers as the sweet, cuddly creatures as they are so often depicted, symbols of nature conservation in Britain!

I should say here again that none of these events had been planned or foreseen; they were accidents arising out of our ignorance of the strength of the badger's territoriality. But we did learn much from these episodes about the forces that operate within a group of badgers and that keep strange animals out. And these early events became especially significant when we looked at them some years later, when we had seen the more subtle aggressive relationships that exist between clan members.

After the early introductions we ended up with a clan of one male, Tim (Fig. 7.3), and the two females, One-Lug and Small, who were sisters and litter mates. In general they got on well, but Small was very much the sub-dominant one. Tim mated with both, although One-Lug tried to pull him off her sister when he mounted her. That was in midsummer and it appeared that we had created the beginnings of a proper clan. But there were more problems to follow.

What we had learned, so far, was that we could not keep strange adult males together, and similarly, we had to keep strange adult females apart. Females did not fight quite as often as males, but the end result was similar. There was little aggression between the sexes. In all of this, the fact that the animals had access to a large enclosure, to different setts, and to separate more-than-ample food supplies made no difference at all; they really went out of their way to seek each other out and fight. And what was also interesting: animals which fought together above ground often slept together in daytime.

Early the following year, on 14 February, One-Lug produced two tiny cubs in the glass-fronted sett. She did not allow anyone near. Two days

FIG. 7.3. The dominant boar in the captive group scratching himself immediately after emerging in the evening, just as wild badgers do.

later, her sister also had two cubs, in a different sleeping chamber. One-Lug hung around, constantly pestering Small; there were growls and loud keckering. A few hours later Small's cubs had gone and One-Lug was with her own cubs again. From that moment, Small's behaviour changed; she became aggressive especially towards her sister. She kept on sitting in the entrance tunnel of One-Lug's chamber, attacking One-Lug and being attacked in return. The next day she obviously obtained what she was after, and we found Small in the natural sett which the badgers had made themselves, inside the enclosure, with one of One-Lug's cubs. The mother herself stayed in her own chamber, with the one remaining offspring.

Days went by, and every time we watched we saw signs of aggression between the two sisters. Since the two families were quite far apart, I hoped that the aggression would die down, but one morning, three weeks later, Small was lying outside the entrance tunnel, bleeding. I put her in a separate cage, stitched her up, filled her with penicillin; two days later she died. One-Lug did not take Small's cub, as I expected; in fact she did not come anywhere near the hole of her late sister. So I decided to intervene again: I managed to take the tiny cub and return it again to One-Lug's chamber.

Our clan was reduced to one boar, one sow, and two cubs, one of each sex. Fortunately, from then on everything else went fine that year. The little cubs Charlie and Jo grew fast; they were delightful to watch and by the autumn they had attained almost adult size. None of the badgers were tame, but Tim and One-Lug were not afraid of people, just rather aggressive. Tim largely ignored his offspring, although he did snap every so often at the male cub, especially during times when One-Lug was in oestrus.

The next year, 14 February 1977, One-Lug again had two cubs: Peter and Valentine. She completely ignored her by now fully grown cubs of the previous year, as did Tim; as long as her present cubs were small she slept with them and apart from the others. All the adult badgers usually slept together, somewhere in one of the many chambers. At night they all went their own way; there were many interactions, of course, but basically the group behaved 'normally'. I will describe some of their behaviour in the following sections. Tim, just as in the previous year, used to snap at the little male cub, Peter, but not any more at Charlie.

The year after that, as soon as One-Lug again produced her now almost traditional two cubs, in the middle of February, she became highly aggressive towards her eldest daughter, Jo. Her younger daughter Val was ignored, but Jo was sought out, harrassed day after day, bitten on the rump and neck. It all happened again; Jo became lethargic and needed medical attention if she were to survive. Regretfully, I took her out of the enclosure to protect her against her own mother. In a wild clan, she would probably have emigrated at that stage.

The story becomes repetitive, but it has to be; the details are important. Another year went by, with more of the same pattern; the clan was growing. Only One-Lug and Tim mated, as far as I knew, and only One-Lug produced a litter, again in the middle of February 1979. Again, the old mother attacked her eldest daughter, Val, again I had to interfere, mending the damage, forcibly taking Val from the group. The males were no problem, and Tim, Charlie, Peter, and Brown got on well. There was a dominance order, corresponding with their respective ages, but there was no obvious aggression. However, when One-Lug was in oestrus, the sons kept out of the way; Tim would attack anything that moved then, especially us, the human observers.

Some time in that summer of 1979, I inadvertently did something which showed that the males were not that tolerant either, despite the lack of overt aggression. I needed one of the badgers for some feeding experiments, away from the others. I took Tim out and returned him a fortnight later. Within hours there was a tremendous fight between him and Charlie, his eldest son. Tim lost. More fighting occurred the next day; later, I found Tim huddled in the far corner of his own territory, with the familiar, horrible wounds, a wreck of a badger. It meant exile for him, too.

Charlie was in charge now, eldest son of the dominant sow. Clearly, there was no point in attempting to introduce an outside male to replace Tim; we just let things be. There were no cubs that next year and virtually no friction between One-Lug and any of her daughters. But one year later, in 1981, two cubs were produced at the usual time, fathered by Charlie. There was a lot of aggression between the oldest females, but this time not so bad that any badger had to be taken out again. The cubs had been fathered by their own brother, but they were perfectly healthy.

Some eight years after we had started with our own clan, we had a well-established badger organization with four adult males, three adult females, and two cubs. Our clan was an extended family. I had twice tried to bring in outside animals, once a male, once a female, carefully, by leaving the strange badger inside a cage within the large badger enclosure. On both occasions the violent attacks and threats from our own local animals towards the newcomers left no doubt that these invaders would not stand any chance of surviving an introduction, and I did not take it further. I had as much evidence as I could get from this one group, that same-sex badgers can only live together within one clan if they are closely related. For firm scientific conclusions, of course, the experiment would need to be repeated several times, but knowing what this would mean in terms of badger aggression and suffering, there was no way in which I could do it again. Nor was this an issue of great priority; after all, it was important to find out what happened in the wild, and we had by then quite a few observations of wild clans to back up our conclusions from the captives.

Also financial problems made it impossible to continue with the captive animals; we had to put a stop to it. That was simple; I just opened the gates of the enclosure. We were lucky to have the badger enclosure in a place where one can do that sort of thing. I thought that the whole general area around the Institute would be perfectly suitable for a good population of badgers; there was lots of food, cover, sites for setts. The reason why there were none already was (I think) that our valley is surrounded by large estates where gamekeepers had kept up an intensive campaign against foxes, snaring and poisoning them. These methods always had captured the badgers first, but fox control had started to relax and I felt that perhaps there was a place for badgers now.

Four of the animals were fitted with a radio-transmitter, the gate of the enclosure was opened, and we stopped providing food. It took four days before any ventured outside and weeks before they started to excavate setts in the slope of the plantations behind the land of the Institute. Food was no problem; we found their scats, faithfully deposited inside the enclosure (where they kept returning), but now full of earthworms. One badger, a yearling sow, disappeared, but the other older female and the two males stayed around, and with the other badgers started two new clans, one next to the Institute's land and one about a mile away. This is three years ago now; several litters have been raised and the area is full of badger activity. Quite often the old, glass-fronted sett in the little badger house is still used by the badgers, now free to come and go as they please.

COMPETITION AND CO-OPERATION BETWEEN MEMBERS OF THE CAPTIVE CLAN

It was clear that even between the closely related badgers there was a fair amount of friction. This expressed itself not only during sexual behaviour; there were also frequent, subtle, aggressive interactions, nothing big, just little snaps, with signs of avoidance, and giving priority of access to food sources. There was a dominance organization behind this and there were indications that these expressions of dominance could well be affected by outside pressures, for instance the amount of food available.

But before looking into that competition further, I wanted to know more about another aspect of the social system which puzzled me. If those aggressive relations within the captive clan were 'normal and natural' (and I thought they were), why would badgers bother to live in clans in the first place? For most of their life, badgers behave in a solitary fashion, foraging and travelling on their own; but they do have a communal territory and the sett is jointly occupied with other badgers with which, obviously, there is a fair amount of friction. What is the point? Why not emigrate into a solitary territory, just as the other Mustelids do? What could be the benefit of group life to a badger?

Probably, such questions ought to be answered in the place where they are posed—in the wild. But there were at least some possibilities that could be followed up in the captive clan. For instance, was there any evidence that badgers communicated over food resources? Or was it possible that some aspect of their denning behaviour, of their joint use of setts, provided group benefits?

The possibility of animals communicating the whereabouts of food resources is not as remote as it might first seem. Very simply, it could be that badgers foraged together, improved their chances of spotting patches of food items, then sharing them. However, we already knew that badgers very rarely moved about in a team, so this possibility was discarded. But in captivity there was some evidence that badgers obtained information from the foraging of others. For instance, we did some experiments in the enclosure with peanuts, a highly favoured food with the badgers. We created rich food patches, and poor ones, which could be recognized as such only when badgers were more or less on top of them. There was no doubt about the result: if a badger found a good patch, it would soon be joined by another, who recognized that there were rich pickings from the behaviour of the first badger. I myself could also see that a badger had struck a good place, merely from the fact that it stayed in one place, eating, whereas at other times it would continue roaming around. In other words, badgers *could* use a joint-foraging strategy, but they just did not do it in the wild. When they did feed together, there was little or no food fighting, or any other obvious signs of aggression.

This, of course, was a very crude test, but the results were unequivocal, at least in captivity. It might well be that in the wild badgers actually used much more subtle means of monitoring each others' foraging successes to their own advantage. It could be that they used their elaborate networks of paths, with all their scent-marks, to obtain information about where clan mates had been foraging. It is a possibility that could be tested in natural experiments; in our enclosure I could not get any further with it.

Another possibility was that an animal might derive a completely different kind of benefit from its clan mates, in the process of protecting itself against the elements, that is keeping warm inside the sett. That might well be very important to badgers; after all, they spend a large part of their lives more or less inactive, deep underground in the sett, just living off their fat reserves.

In our badger house we could see what happened underground, who slept with whom and where. There were eight different chambers where badgers could sleep, and if snuggling up to another badger were important to them, we should find that they would sleep together more often than if they were just sleeping in chambers randomly. And we would have to make sure that if we found badgers asleep in the same chamber, it was not just because they preferred that particular place to curl up in, but because it was other badgers that attracted them.

We analysed the data for the first few years in the history of our enclosure. There was no doubt that badgers slept together much more often than could be expected by chance and that they did so not just because they all happened to favour the same chamber—they sought each other out. The more dominant a badger, the more often it slept with others, but a sow with cubs kept well away. The most unpopular badger, the one that was chased and attacked most often, was also the one that slept alone most often. Yet, even such an outcast would often sleep next to its worst enemy. This communal sleeping, therefore, appeared to be really important to the animals; most likely just to keep warm. I did not try to correlate this tendency to sleep together with outside temperatures, as perhaps I should have done. However, if we leave the activities of the breeding female, One-Lug, out of it, the badgers slept together most often between October and March and far less often in summer. It seems that with this huddling habit we have at least one clear advantage that badgers might derive from their clan association.

In fact, sleeping together may well be the most important of such group benefits in badger society. As I indicated above, there was little in their foraging that suggested a beneficial, co-operative approach to increase efficiency, nor have I been able to detect this in any other aspect of their behaviour. Badgers seemed to be mostly remarkably asocial animals, as soon as they were away from their sleeping chambers.

As just one more example of this, the species did not appear to have any alarm signal which could help clan members when there was an enemy about. On many occasions when I was watching my captives feed together, all eight or nine of them slowly milling around in an area a few metres square, some badger right at the back or in the middle might see me or smell me. Just like any wild badger they would then dash off, but the neighbouring badgers would not be aware of any trouble and they were left at the mercy of what could have been serious danger. I had, in fact, been in similar situations in the wild. If these animals had been mongooses, spotted hyaenas, or wolves there would always had been a distinctive alarm call from the first animal to spot the danger.

From these observations it would appear that the immediate benefits which an animal derived from living in a clan, as distinct from living in a solitary system, were small. Moreover, there were also disadvantages to group life, for instance the competition between badgers in close proximity.

I have already mentioned aggression between them, the fact that some (usually the older) individuals dominate others; it is especially important to know whether this is in any way linked to the availability of resources. If badgers within the clan fight to the extent that some of them might be forced to emigrate, or even be killed, would they do so more if there is little food, or few places for setts, or a scarcity of whatever else may be important to them?

We decided to look at this question in the captive clan with regard to the presence of food, mostly because in the wild that appeared to be a likely limiting factor in our study areas. Our badgers got most of their food from us in the form of dead day-old chicks, or rabbits, supplemented with peanuts and barley; to this they themselves added whatever natural food they could scrape out of the enclosure. If we gave them a week of just a few peanuts and the odd dead rabbit, we called that their starvation diet; we compared their behaviour to each other during such lean weeks with that during weeks of plenty. I should stress that during such lean periods badgers probably ate no less than during many such periods in the wild; like many carnivores they naturally live on a feast or famine regime, and their large fat reserves (especially in winter) must be an adaptive feature related to this. Thus, during just a few lean days, we should not expect any major adjustments to their numbers or organization. On the other hand if, in the wild in the long term, food were to exercise an important effect on numbers of badgers in a clan then we might see over such short periods as our captivity observations subtle changes in the relationships between animals which could indicate the mechanism of badger adjustments.

This was exactly what happened. A student, Gill Radcliffe, counted the occurrences of different kinds of interaction between the badgers, during four-hour watches in lean and fat periods (15 days each). When badgers had to search hard for their food, she saw an average of 1.8 real physical clashes per evening between them and she heard 5.4 growls. But when they were replete there was far less trouble: she only saw 0.2 clashes per evening then and she heard 1.7 growls. This was a highly significant difference, but the other, non-aggressive behaviour patterns remained more or less the same. It was not as if these badgers fought over food when there was less to go round; there was an overall difference in the relations between the animals, which showed on all sorts of occasions.

When another student, Grahame Pierce, wanted to repeat these observations a year later, we ran into trouble, because of the badgers' sexual behaviour. The results initially were comparable to what we had seen before, but then One-Lug went into oestrus. This was in the middle of the summer and she had already mated several times that year, as badgers do. In our captive group, the immediate consequence of a female in oestrus was always that the dominant male became exceedingly aggressive to the other males, to outsiders, to any of us coming close to the enclosure. This lasted for about a week and, of course, it completely upset our observation schedule. We planned to do some proper experiments on this topic during the following year, but for various reasons this did not materialize. Despite such complications, the results of these preliminary observations were quite clear cut: when food was short, aggression increased. And it was aggression between the badgers which made it necessary for us to remove badgers from the group, as related above. I would speculate that this is the mechanism which operates in the wild, that it is the level of aggression between clan members which puts pressure on individuals to leave, to emigrate to an uncertain fate, and that this level of aggression is affected by the available resources.

Another probable consequence to a badger of living in a group is the fact that only few animals reproduce. In our captive clan only One-Lug, one of the two original founding sisters of the clan, produced all the offspring, and probably only one male was involved at a time. Badgers are sexually mature by the age of one, so there must have been other reasons why no more litters were produced. In at least one case One-Lug killed her sister's litter, and I suspected infanticide on a second occasion. But I was quite certain that in the other years, when there were three or four other females in addition to One-Lug, a different inhibiting mechanism was responsible and the others did not give birth at all. In the wild something similar also occurs and clans with several simultaneous litters of cubs are relatively rare (Chapter 8).

Perhaps this is as far as observations on captive animals can go; they may generate ideas which can be tested by experiments. We learned from our observations about the deleterious effects of aggression, the inhibitions on reproduction, and about the possible benefits of group life: the warmth derived from huddling in the sleeping chambers, the joint efforts of digging holes and lining them with bedding. They even indicated potential benefits which badgers do not take up in the wild, that is information derived from each other during joint foraging. But, by design, the badgers in the enclosure could never give us any clues about the dangers of leaving a clan. It may well be that this is the crux of their spatial organization; only wild badgers can tell us more about that.

Further details

See Kruuk *et al.* (1986).

8

Social organization

Our Speyside study area was the setting for a typical badger population, with badgers neither too sparse nor too dense. It was an area rich in species of birds and mammals, a loch surrounded by huge birches, with osprey overhead, roe-deer barking on the slopes, and wildcats and pine martens. The badger setts were about half a mile apart, with the huge sandy spoil heaps against the slopes, every badger clan in its own area, demarcated by a conspicuous boundary. It was like a map of countries, and they can be thought of in almost the same way, in terms of numbers of inhabitants, relations between the clans, their aggression, and their sources of subsistence. The captive badgers in Banchory had been a great help in understanding what happened within these boundaries and how the clan was organized as a community. But the captives were useful only because I could compare them with what happened in the wild in Speyside, where I knew several individuals over the years and where I could compare their interactions, and I could hear from the bleeps on my radio-receiver who was sleeping where. With these observations a social structure emerged, a picture of relations between individuals within the clan.

Badger clans have a complicated social system, which was not at all obvious when we were following and watching them, because of the animals' curiously solitary existence within the clan. Follow a troup of baboons, or a pack of wolves or hyaenas, and the existence of complicated clans or groups and of their social structure is immediately obvious, and part of the animals' day-to-day life. But to stay with a badger for a few nights is to stay with a loner, an animal that avoids its own kind rather than socializes, where the first impression is of a social structure of a unit of one. This may be difficult to appreciate if badgers have only been watched on their sett and their 'friendly' interactions observed in front of the entrances (Figs 8.1, 8.3, 8.4, 8.5). That is at the most for only a short while on any particular day and often involves the cubs; but more frequently a badger just slips out of the sett into the range and the vast loneliness of the night. Following badgers during radio-tracking one gets the strong impression that they are completely solitary.

The social organization within the clan must be partly the result of

Fig. 8.1. Cubs and adults of various ages grooming and playing. They are gregarious in front of the sett, but solitary when they leave to forage. (Photograph by R. Tanner.)

meetings, often brief ones, at the sett and anywhere in the territory. It must be partly the result also of the experience of badgers on their own in the range, of their ability to scrape a living together. Somehow, all this causes some badgers to stay, others to emigrate, and some to reproduce. In the observations in Wytham and the various Scottish study areas we began to get some idea about the rules underlying the badger system, about what a clan consisted of, about the relations between the sexes, who reared the cubs. They were the rules of a contradiction, of a tight community of solitary animals.

Normally, a clan consisted of boars and sows, often several of each. These were animals of an age when they would be sexually mature, and then there were the cubs, the young of the year. One thing that had fascinated me in the study in Wytham was a 'clan' of males only there, a bachelor group, squeezed in between the normal clans. It was the only group of bachelors in the small samples of clans that I could look at, but it seemed a good solution to a problem of surplus animals. There were six males, perhaps outcasts: two very old ones, three young ones (one or two years old), and only one, 'normal', middle-aged animal, but he had had his nose bitten off; in fact all were pretty scarred. They had a very small territory, about 20 hectares, very long and thin, between the territories of two, other, large clans. In the other, more normal clans in Wytham the sex ratio was about equal, as it was in Speyside.

I have never come across another bachelor club like that, nor have others like Chris Cheeseman in the Cotswolds, who has caught and marked many more badgers than I have. It must have been a very unusual situation; a pity, because it was such a neat system, reminiscent of the bachelor herds of antelopes or deer. However, after I had finished the main study in Speyside in Scotland, Paul Latour, my PhD student who continued there, found something similar. He happened to catch and radio-track one badger male which spent both years of his study in a small area right on the border between two clans, without female company. So perhaps such animals do occur more commonly, but it could well be that for some reason we rarely caught them.

The centre of the clan territory, the large main sett, was the place where individuals met, often spent the day, and where the cubs stayed. The sett was dug as a communal effort, with the result passed down the generations. As in their other activities, the actual digging was done solitarily and animals did not help each other by working simultaneously. At any time of the night, an individual could suddenly appear at the entrance of the sett, walking backwards, dragging a heap of earth. I noticed that almost all badgers took part in the digging, irrespective of sex or age. But it appeared that the older, more dominant badgers were more involved than young ones, and they also spent more time there. In Wytham, it was striking that three, large, adult boars always spent the day in the main sett, whereas a younger male and three adult females were away in smaller outlying holes during about half the days that I checked.

But the main sett was the place where the cubs were born and perhaps it was just this presence of cubs that made the sett such a focal point. Cubs were very conspicuous, especially when they were a few months old. They often came out in daylight, and sometimes it was not difficult to get them to accept food, almost from our hands. They romped around and played, and we, as did generations of other badger watchers, spent endless evenings with them. It was their very conspicuousness which often concealed a point that could be very important: there usually were, in fact, very few cubs, and this touches on a question which is of fundamental importance in badger society.

It is known that badgers can be sexually mature when they are about one year old, males somewhat earlier than females. In theory, every female could produce her first litter of cubs around her second birthday, in February, and then every year thereafter. But this did not happen; something prevented reproduction in most of the sows. For instance, in

Speyside we caught 28 different adult females in the March–June period, some of them over several subsequent years, altogether 57 times (ignoring occasions when we caught them more than once in the same year). Only 38 per cent were lactating, about one-third. This had also been found elsewhere, in England and in Sweden. What happened, in fact, was that usually only one sow in each clan produced a litter, irrespective of how many badgers there were in the clan (Fig. 8.2). There were quite a few exceptions to this 'rule' (Figs 8.3, 8.5) and some observers have seen as many as three different litters together. But such cases were unusual; a normal average clan had only one litter each year.

Moreover, we had good evidence that that one litter was produced by the same female in subsequent years. Every spring we spent many days on a big round-up of badgers with our traps, and we found particular sows that were lactating, the same ones as the year before, as well as other females which were dry. There was one old female which was at least eight years old at the end of the study and which we had caught every single year of her adult life, always dry: she never lactated and therefore never bred. In the same group, the main Loch clan, one other female produced a litter in the two first years we were there, but she disappeared, and for one year there were no cubs in the beautiful birch woods on the slope immediately above the loch. Then, the year after that, another one of the females turned up in our traps with a heavy udder; she had two cubs, and that same sow repeated this the following and last year of the study.

This kind of observation repeated itself several times in the other clans. Against that background the data from the captive clan became useful

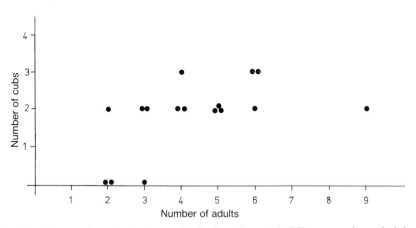

FIG. 8.2. The number of cubs observed in badger clans with different numbers of adults, Speyside, April–June 1977–82. Cubs are usually about two months old when first seen above ground (from Kruuk and Parish 1987).

again; most likely, only the dominant female in a clan was the mother of the cubs, and the other subordinate females did not reproduce.

The crucial question, of course, was what exactly did happen to create this result? Did only certain sows, the dominant ones, get pregnant, or did some females lose their litter either before birth or immediately after birth? At this point we needed physiological information; from our own observations there was no way of providing answers. Some clues came from the badgers in captivity; there, we had seen that one of the other females in the group gave birth, but lost the litter almost immediately, very likely to the sharp teeth of the dominant sow. This, quite probably, could also happen in the wild, but equally likely it was not the whole explanation.

For instance, we also saw that there was some competition between females at the time of copulation. This expressed itself in several ways; at its most severe, the dominant female in captivity pulled a male, who was mounting another female, off his mate. In one of our wild clans, a large group at New Deer, two females which always slept together in the same chamber stayed a long distance apart for a whole week, during the time that one of them was in oestrus and had mated with the dominant boar. There were also aggressive growls between them at that time when they were above ground on the sett.

FIG. 8.3. Young non-lactating sow, old boar (centre foreground), three cubs, and two other badgers at the sett entrance. (Photograph by R. Tanner.)

Whilst we were working on the badgers in Scotland, there was another, very important study going on in Sweden. Hans Ahnlund concentrated his attention on the problem of badger reproduction, and because he was able to dissect a large number of carcasses he came up with some fascinating information which was directly relevant to our questions. For instance, he discovered that, at least in Sweden, virtually all female badgers two years old and over became pregnant, as well as about half of the yearlings— whatever mechanism was interfering with the process of multiplication, this must have happened some time around birth or fairly soon after. The difficulty, of course, was that we could not see what happened inside the sett. Behavioural interference of badger sows with each others' litters could therefore be widespread, but we do not know. At the same time, having seen our captive clan at close quarters over several years, I think it was unlikely that all, or even most, of the sows there were impregnated by their father or brothers. There was virtually no sexual interaction between badgers so closely related during the times that they were observed, but there was a lot of sexual behaviour between the two dominant animals.

The evidence was by no means conclusive, but at least very suggestive: under captive conditions there was a strong sexual inhibition between badgers other than the dominant pair. This could be an incest-taboo or some other mechanism. It could be that in the wild sub-dominants copulated with a member of a neighbouring clan. Of course this is highly speculative, but it would make sense in the clans where everybody seemed related to everybody else, except for the oldest boar and sow which were not related to each other.

Another aspect of the badger sexual organization which Hans Ahnlund studied in detail was the strange phenomenon of delayed implantation, with its various curious corollaries. His findings have several implications for our understanding of the badger social organization, and I will describe some of his results. The fact that badgers have a delayed implantation has been known for a long time. Without going into the physiological details, it means that the foetus can start developing long after fertilization took place, at a suitable time of the year. In the case of badgers, late winter appears to be the optimal season for giving birth, and with a gestation period of about two months this means that foetal development has to start some time during early or midwinter. Clearly, food availability for badgers at that time is very low, which makes those months unsuitable for accommodating all the activities associated with mating. In fact, badgers are extremely inactive then, not quite hibernating, but almost. Delayed implantation enables mating to take place at any time during the year, with embryo development arrested at a very early stage and not starting properly until some time in December.

Fig. 8.4. Young adult badger about to leave the sett area to forage. Cubs and others in background. (Photograph by R. Tanner.)

It is a simple system: mate during a suitable time of year, then implant in the right month for birth at the right time. There are several species of mammals which have opted for this convenient adaptation, but badgers appear to have taken the process a few steps further. Ahnlund showed that badgers mate mostly early in spring, very soon after the cubs are born, during the post-partem oestrus period. But then the females continue to ovulate right throughout the year into the autumn, irrespective of whether they have mated during that year or not. So the number of fertilized ova (blastocysts) in a sow increases over the months, and by the middle of the summer a 'saturation level' has been reached, i.e. almost all sows which are going to be mated that year will be pregnant and each sow carries as many blastocysts as she is going to carry.

The social consequences of this arrangement are profound. First, it means that one litter may have been fathered by several different boars. Second, productive mating can occur for a long time of the year, so even if a badger male has copulated with his clan sow(s) during early spring, he should maintain his sexual activities later in the year and he has to prevent cuckoldry at all times. The sow's periods of oestrus are accompanied by a

FIG. 8.5. Five cubs at play, with one (probably young) adult in top right of picture. Note the long claws. The cubs must be from at least two different litters. (Photograph by R. Tanner.)

great deal of aggression from the boar towards outsiders, at least in our captive group. This happened even, or perhaps especially, when the sow did not allow the boar to copulate; perhaps the sow's condition kept his testosteron flowing at high levels, causing high aggression? The effect following on from that may be that the male makes more effort to drive strangers out of the clan territory.

The physiological observations in Sweden therefore suggest that the badgers' sexual organization, especially the repeated periods of oestrus of the sows, may have a bonding function, with effects far beyond mere reproduction. The advantages of such a possible bonding are not immediately clear. Badger males do not contribute directly to the provision of their offspring, so there is little gain for the badger sow in having a boar 'faithful' to her. But it could be, and this is pure speculation, that it would be advantageous for a sow to have a boar which keeps strange badgers away, either because they are an extra drain on the resources of the territory, or because they could be a threat to her offspring. To illustrate this last point, there are many carnivores in which infanticide is known, especially by males. Hyaenas are one example, lions another, and there are many more.

But I should stress again that this is no more than speculation; we do not have the information to draw any definite conclusions.

Returning to the question of why usually no more than one sow produces a litter in each clan, it would obviously be highly instructive to look at exactly what happens in those clans which do manage to rear more than one litter. How do those few second, or even third, litters manage to survive? Perhaps it happens in those territories where there are several suitable setts, instead of the usual one main sett and several 'outliers'. In our various study areas we only had two cases of multiple litters and both were in large clans (one with six and one with nine adults), with very extensive setts, and each with at least a dozen outliers. Perhaps females manage to rear their litters well apart from each other, at least for the first few weeks; later, the cubs from the two litters may join and play together, and the relationship appears to be harmonious once the cubs are large enough.

There are several species of carnivores where young from previous litters help in the rearing of their mothers' offspring during the following year(s). These helpers have stimulated a great deal of interest from students of animal behaviour, with the obvious question: why do they do it? Jackals, foxes, lions, wolves, hyaenas, and many others often spend one or more years at home, taking food to their younger siblings, instead of going off to rear their own broods. In several cases it has been shown that more young survive in litters of mothers with helpers, and the more helpers the better. It has even been demonstrated that more young survive in one litter with a helper than in two separate litters with no helpers. This sounds very convincing, but it is circumstantial; I am not aware of any studies which demonstrated unequivocally that helpers really do help. It is always possible that good territories or good parents keep cubs at home for an extra year or longer and that these same territories or parents also produce more cubs next year, irrespective of whether they are being assisted by previous offspring or not.

With the observations on helping in other species in mind, I looked closely at what was happening in the badger clans. Do older siblings bring food to younger cubs, and if so, does it really help? They were fascinating questions and uncomfortably easy to answer: we never saw any sign of any helping whatsoever. Perhaps that was not surprising in a species like the badger, because even the mother of the young cubs never, or hardly ever, provided them with any food apart from her own milk. Very occasionally we saw a sow carry a piece of rabbit or some other meat into the sett (Plate 19), but basically the dependent cubs were suckled only, for about three or four months of their life. Quite likely, this was caused by the fact that badgers fed on small prey such as earthworms, hardly the kind of morsels that make provisioning an easy and efficient option for such a large animal.

None of the males, either the dominant male or any of the others, were ever seen to help with provisioning or to walk around with the cubs. They might play with them on the sett when the cubs were still rather small and they would scent-mark them, but there was no obvious contribution to their immediate survival. All parental care came from the female on her own, from the mother.

These observations suggest that, at least in the case of the badger, the reason why young animals did not immediately disperse to start breeding somewhere else was not that it would be more advantageous for the propagation of their genes for them to stay at home and contribute to the provision of their siblings.

Once the cubs began to move about the territory, they first went with their mother and no other badger was involved. We met those parties, worming somewhere in a pasture or between the trees, mother and young fairly close together. But after June this kind of sight was fairly rare; we still frequently saw just the cubs together and for several months in the summer they appeared to operate as a small gang. The mother went her own way then, foraging on her own. But from late summer onwards each cub began to move about on its own, finding its own food independently of others, and they had become the same solitary foragers as the rest of the clan. Then, after their first winter, when they were, or at least could be, sexually mature, began the time when they had the option either of staying in their natal clan, on known ground with all its advantages but where they might not be able to breed, or of emigrating.

DISPERSAL

The observation of dispersing animals is notoriously difficult and there are few species of mammal in which we have good observations on exactly what happens when an animal leaves its natal range and where it settles down. In badgers such observations are even more difficult, because many animals do not move until they are several years old, if they move at all. Over the years we have been able to document a few cases in the Speyside study area.

In September 1979 a small, frightened badger cub walked into one of our traps, in one of the central clan ranges, the Sheilich. He was a little runt of a badger, perhaps born late, and at the time I did not put his chances of survival very high. The Sheilich was a good, healthy clan, with five adults; the dominant boar was the very old Cauliflower. The young badger received his tattoo in the usual place, the loin, and we released him again inside the sett next to the trap. He was registered in our card-system, but we did not expect to see much more of him. In June of the next year we were trapping again, and there he turned up in a trap not too far from the previous one. But he had changed almost beyond recognition: he was now a strong young male, and furiously aggressive, charging at anyone who came close to the trap. That kind of behaviour is very unusual for a badger; they tend to sit quietly inside their temporary confinement. I only recognized him after I had darted and immobilized him, and the tattoo left no doubt about his identity. And whilst I looked at his tattoo, I noticed a peculiarity: he was in perfect order, but he only had one testicle. His nickname was to be Hitler.

Twice more that year he walked into a trap, where he fed on the peanut bait, and responded in his same aggressive manner as soon as we approached the trap. He carried a radio-transmitter, and often came to the barn of the farm where we stayed, which was in the Sheilich range, where he fed on the heaps of barley, or where he shredded the bags of feed cubes meant for the sheep. He was a normal, regular member of the clan, an adult, sexually mature male, living in the territory also occupied by his father Cauliflower. The year after that, when he was about two years old, things changed.

His radio had stopped functioning by then, and it was a complete surprise when we caught him, in May, in the centre of the next-door territory, the main Loch clan. But this time he looked different again—he was now a battered badger, scarred, thin, with large wounds on his rump and in his neck. Yet, he was still full of aggression. After we put another transmitter on him, we found that he used that main Loch range as if he had always been there, with just the occasional foray to the barn in Sheilich, but otherwise respecting the main Loch boundaries exactly as all other clan members did. There was no sign of the male who had been in his new range before that time, nor did we see or catch any other males there. All evidence was that Hitler had taken over, and had become the resident male of the main Loch clan.

In this observation a young and subordinate male from one clan had taken over the range of a neighbouring clan, and there was no sign of another resident male in that new range. During the five years that we studied the Speyside badgers intensively, we recorded six occasions when a male moved from one clan range to that of a neighbour, out of the 23 cases where we caught males in at least two subsequent years. We never saw an animal move to a range further away; it was always that of a neighbour. And in all cases we were reasonably confident that the male which moved came from a range where there were one or more other males, usually older. We never had a male which was obviously born into a range, subsequently becoming the oldest and presumably dominant one in that territory.

Of course, this is not exactly a massive body of evidence, but I think it is sufficient for a generalization: when a badger male matures, he does not just take off and roam around, but stays at home for as long as it takes to move into a vacancy next door. Or, perhaps, until he is evicted by his own family or a new usurper, something which we speculated must happen, but which we never observed. All boars which emigrated were mature: one was two years old (the example I related above), one was an estimated 2–3 years old, and the others were four years old or over, as estimated from tooth wear.

We never saw any female badgers move from one clan to another: they stayed where they were born, or sometimes expanded their range into a vacant one. But they never really emigrated. An example of range expansion is the following.

A young sow from the Milton Clan was first caught in 1977, when probably about two years old. She was radio-tracked over three years, and in the first of those years stayed neatly in the Milton area, respecting the clan boundaries, sleeping in the main sett, foraging in the same, central pastures that other Milton badgers used. But in the second year of our observations, in 1978, we first found her in the headquarters of the neighbours, the Sheilich clan, later again in the Milton sett, and she continued to alternate between them: a few days here, a few days next door. She foraged in her native Milton range, but also in that half of the Sheilich range which bordered on Milton. What was especially interesting was that there was another female around in the Sheilich range, and also one in Milton, and both these other sows were breeding. In the third year that we followed our Milton/Sheilich female she continued as she had done in the previous year, using both ranges; then she abruptly disappeared, and we presumed that she had died, perhaps on the road through the two territories.

This female was one of two sows which we saw expand their range, out of 37 which we knew over at least two years. None of them ever took up residence elsewhere in the study area, as we had seen of the males. But range expansion also occurred in males (two observations), so that was a phenomenon common to both sexes.

These individual moves, the range expansion of females or the emigration or expansion of males, occurred at various times throughout our study. There was no indication that this happened in any way more frequently in the later years, when food stress was more in evidence. To me, this suggested that such moves are probably not in response to changes in environmental conditions, but are clearly of great social significance. It is, in fact, known for many species of animal that the males move when maturing and the females may either stay in their mothers' range or make a move smaller than that of the males. Badgers appear to fit into that pattern very neatly, only they seem to postpone a move for longer, up to several years, than most other animals.

However, it is strange that almost all badgers of both sexes in the high-density areas of southern England appear to stay at home, whatever the age or reproductive state; this was reported by Chris Cheeseman. Perhaps they have a quite different social system, either with much more inbreeding or with males moving across territorial boundaries to mate with neighbouring females, then returning again to their own range. The mating systems of badgers in different densities should make a very rewarding study.

Whilst the moves of individuals between territories in our Scottish study area may have been independent of changes in food availability, there were other things going on which seemed to be a consequence of the increasing hardship amongst the Speyside badgers. I have already mentioned the increase there in the proportion of the clan range used by individual badgers, from an average 45 to 75 per cent (Chapter 6), but there were also changes in their social behaviour, in their gregariousness. Despite the fact that ranges of individual badgers overlapped with each other more at the end than at the beginning of the five-year study, the animals became less social in their sleeping habits, at least in one and probably in two of the large clans. Whereas early on in 1976 in Speyside I would have characterized the social arrangement as one in which most badgers used the central sett and foraged from there in different directions, later each individual in these large clans was more inclined to have its own 'outlier' sett. In the Fish Farm clan, close to Aviemore, the females which we radio-tagged in 1978 spent 81 per cent of their day in the huge main sett, but in 1982 this was only 37 per cent. The rest of the time they were long distances away, in small setts, usually on their own. It seemed likely that this clan was on the verge of breaking up into small components. Unfortunately we were not able to continue the study for long enough to find out.

What alerted me to the implications of such a possible break-up was an almost simultaneous study by one of my students, Giorgio Pigozzi, on badgers in Italy. There, in a dry, Mediterranean habitat, without earthworms, badgers were solitary animals, scraping a living from the scattered populations of insects and various fruits. There was almost no recognizable clan structure and the badgers appeared to be organized like any other, 'average', solitary, Mustelid carnivore. A comparison with the Speyside observations was almost irresistible: once the highly patchy supply of earthworms in Speyside decreased, the clan structure appeared to disintegrate.

One general implication of our observations on the various changes and variations is that the social structure of the badger appears to be fairly adaptable. The system of possible movements of individuals from one clan to another, of adjustable gregariousness within clans, variations in individual and clan ranges and their overlap, all played a part in the adjustment of badger society to changing conditions. We could not do any experiments, so it was not possible to say categorically what, in all these changes, was actually caused by the agricultural upheavals and what was part of the badgers' normal 'social turnover', the normal system of responses to alternatives which makes the adjustment to environmental change possible. But whichever way this worked, the observations did show that the system is nowhere near as rigid as we originally thought.

Further details

See Kruuk (1978*a*, 1986, 1987); Kruuk and Parish (1987). See also Anderson and
Trewhella (1985); Ahnlund (1980); Neal and Harrison (1958); Cheeseman *et
al.* (1988); Harris and Cresswell (1987); Macdonald and Moehlman (1983);
Pigozzi (1987); Powell (1979).

9

Observations on communication

After having watched quite a few carnivores, such as different species of cats, dogs, hyaenas, and others, I was struck by the lack of diversity in postures and behaviour patterns which played a role in the badgers' social communication. Their communication was not at all obvious and the signals appeared to have a quite different meaning from similar ones used by other carnivore families. A wagging tail, a scratching paw, a crouching figure, a growl—it all meant something quite different when it came from a badger. I had to learn this to my cost, initially; through my ignorance of badger communication I did not recognize that I was being threatened by a boar in our captive group, which then attacked in earnest.

In that particular case, the visual threat signals consisted of quick flicks of the tail and of scraping with the hind legs, which were both signs of extreme aggression. There must have been scent signals, too, which I also could not recognize because I lacked the olfactory equipment. This, clearly, was a big problem: a great deal of badger communication occurred through their noses, and we had no immediate way of appreciating that. A badger's nose is very complicated, with a large labyrinth of passages; it must have an enormous capacity for detecting and distinguishing smells. The animals also have scent glands over many parts of the body, not just under the tail. Communication, which we cannot detect, takes place through these glands. It is not just as if someone is speaking in a language we do not understand, it is as if we were sitting with our eyes closed whilst people around us communicated by sign language. However, there is some light in this darkness. There are a few visible behaviour patterns associated with scent communication and we can analyse some of the glandular secretions in the laboratory. But we must assume that most of the badgers' olfactory communication goes completely undetected.

Before describing our observations on the role of scent, I should say something more about other aspects of badger communication, first of all about visual signals. Some of these were of immediate relevance to our work. For instance, we had to be able to recognize aggression to interpret possible rank orders and interactions between animals which were important in their organization within the clan, and between clans. But other aspects of their behaviour, or rather of their appearance, were less relevant to our main questions, although just as interesting.

For instance, the stripes on the badger face. Many naturalists have wondered what their social significance could be and why badgers do not have a plain face. Almost 80 years ago it was suggested that the stripes had a warning function. The question then arises as to why other animals do not use this sort of coloration, foxes, for instance, or honey badgers. So we continued the speculations of others. One immediately relevant observation is that the stripes are exactly the same in males and females. It is extremely difficult to tell the sex of a badger just from its face; a boar is somewhat broader in the jaw, but there have been many times when I was wrong in my determined attempts to sex badgers that way. On several occasions I have had a badger in a trap and confidently told bystanders that we had caught a sow, judging by the head, only to be confronted by irrefutable evidence to the contrary after anaesthetizing the animal. Some large boars had a quite unmistakeable head, but many I found difficult to identify as males—and I know that this happened to other acknowledged experts, too.

If it is unlikely that there is any sexual significance in the striped face, could the stripes perhaps serve the purpose of accentuating any aggressive signals? One of my students did some simple experiments with the captive badgers, experiments which gave no decisive answers but at least provided some clues. Carol Oakley presented some members of the captive group with cardboard shapes of a badger head, with different facial patterns. For this she used a short tunnel sticking out from the side of the enclosure, in which badgers could find food and at the end of which she could present her model attached to a stick, from above. So a badger walking into the tunnel would see a face at the other end, a face that could be black, or white, or white with horizontal black stripes, or white with vertical black stripes, like a proper badger's face. The badger could not see or smell the observer, who was well above the tunnel on a platform. The observer could move the model when the badger was near it, to make it seem alive, but during the experiment she did not know with which of the models the badger was confronted, although she could see the badger itself. The models were presented in a random sequence of 20 minute trials (Fig. 9.1).

The only two animals on which Carol got enough observations in the time available to her were two adult boars, one of them the dominant animal in the clan, Tim. But with these two the results were quite unambiguous: both attacked the model with the vertical black stripes (i.e. the badger face) significantly more than any other model. When the results were expressed as numbers of bites per hour of presentation, the black face received 0.3, the white one 0, the horizontal stripes 0.4, and the vertical

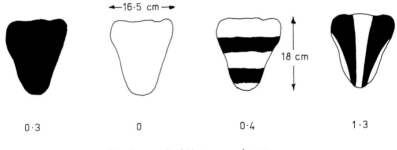

Number of bites per hour

FIG. 9.1. Cardboard models used in experiments with captive badgers and the aggression they released in two adult males (as number of biting attacks per hour).

stripes 1.3; the total time that badgers were confronted with each model was about 7 hours. Or, to express the results in different terms, the badger face was attacked in 10 of the 25 trials, while all the others together were attacked only 6 times in 61 trials ($\chi^2 = 8.76$, $p < 0.001$). Carol also looked at other behaviour patterns of the badger towards the model, but saw no great differences, except in the rate of scent marking, which was also higher when the model with vertical stripes was shown.

These simple experiments still did not tell us why badgers should have a striped face; the results might mean merely that the badger recognized the model as that of a face of a conspecific. I think that the very conspicuous pattern is useful to badgers in their uniquely large underground tunnel system, where it must be almost completely dark, and only a highly striking pattern could show to warn of an approach and prevent collisions and associated aggression.

The results of our experiments perhaps took us somewhat closer to an understanding of some of the head movements of badgers. Amongst the few visual signals which badgers used, positions of and movements with the head were important. There was a very striking stance, used almost only by males, which we called the Upright (Plate 1). It was a rather aggressive posture, used by dominant animals, often just before rushing towards a possible opponent, and showing the face full on. It was remarkably similar to a posture of the same name, used by many birds, in the same context; by gulls, for instance. There it was named Upright by Niko Tinbergen, who recognized it as an aggressive signal. Very interestingly, he suggested that the facial mask of a black-headed gull had evolved in order to accentuate postures such as the Upright. That gull displays a full-frontal Upright in a more exaggerated form than other gulls, and in the breeding season it has a striking brown face, against a white neck.

The complete opposite of the Upright in both form and function was the Curl-up, when a badger of either sex put its head between its forelegs with its forehead on the ground. It was hiding all its vulnerable parts, and it was also hiding the conspicuous stripes; this was the position of a badger under extreme threat. Animals did it when they were very frightened, for instance when caught in a trap or in a snare (Fig. 2.3), or when they were attacked and overcome by another badger, and cornered. Clearly this was a very effective way of coping with an attack on the body, for it should protect eyes, ears, throat, and other vulnerable parts. What was especially interesting to me, however, was that so few other species of carnivore showed this posture: if it was so useful to shield eyes, ears, and throat, why did a fox or a cat or a hyaena not do it? Perhaps because it is that they did not have any conspicuous stripes to hide, which is the outstanding feature of the badger head. Again, in exactly the same way Niko Tinbergen found that black-headed gulls turn their face-mask away as an appeasement gesture; other gulls do this, too, but nowhere near as often or as strikingly.

In another defensive posture a badger kept facing an opponent, but with its head low to the ground, so that the animal was almost crouching: we called this the Forward stance (Fig. 9.2). It was very common in aggressive encounters between males as well as between females. Frequently the badger growled, or 'keckered' (see below), and it was likely to bite back hard when attacked in this posture (unlike the Curl-up, in which posture

Fig. 9.2. Forward posture by a female (left) directed at a male badger.

badgers never actively defended themselves, but just adopted it for protection).

There was one more, striking visual display which needs to be mentioned. This was Pilo-erection, where a badger would put either all its hair on end, or else only that of its tail (like a bottle-brush), or the hair on its hindquarters (Fig. 9.3). I have not seen this in the reactions of one badger to another; it occurred mostly in cubs, when they were suddenly frightened by something, and it made them look about twice their real size.

This was almost the whole repertoire of displays, of visual signs; a poor one, by any standards. There were some other postures and movements, especially involving the tail, which I will discuss later (the reason why I do not detail them here is that they were probably much more related to olfactory than visual displays). But there was one more group of behaviour patterns which occurred often in conjunction with visual displays and postures—the badgers' sounds.

No one has yet attempted to make an inventory of the badger's repertoire of calls, which is not really surprising. First, the animals are not very vocal and, second, whenever they do make themselves heard it is difficult to classify the various noises. There were no two kinds of sound the badgers made which did not have some intermediates as well, and it was almost

FIG. 9.3. Pilo-erection in a large cub, in a sudden fright.

impossible to describe one of their utterances as a wail and another, slightly different one as a growl. One call grades into the next, in a continuum of soft growls, and grunts and yells. I will describe a few, more or less clear-cut sounds and situations, mostly because they give an idea of the kind of information that we ourselves used to recognize the interactions between animals. But I am aware of the inadequacy of such a description.

The same quality that made these sounds so difficult to describe would also give the animals access to a huge variety of subtle expressions. A sound continuum is a better basis for communication than a few discrete calls, except, perhaps, in situations where messages have to be simple and unambiguous, such as in long-distance calls. But badgers did not have anything that could be used for long-distance communication, as do foxes or lions or hyaenas, for instance. These species use calls which can be heard literally miles away, calls which are so characteristic that for naturalists they are an indispensible part of the English woodlands or the African bush. Their messages are simple and an important part of their social fabric. Badgers have been reported to produce extremely loud screams, but no one has yet described actually *seeing* a badger do this, and no one in our group ever heard any such loud noises in many hundreds of hours of observation. I believe other animals must have been responsible for these reports, perhaps foxes.

Another type of sound which was very conspicuous because of its absence in badgers was an alarm call. This was something that struck me very forcibly: the total lack of any means of warning other clan members of trouble, especially since alarm calls are so well developed in other species. Watch a crowd of hyaenas eating at a carcass in Africa and suddenly you may hear a soft, staccato series of grunts from an animal that happens to be looking up. The immediate effect is that all hyaenas scatter, as fast as they can, without even attempting to identify the cause of concern. If it was a lion, as often happened, there might be no time for contemplation: they have to run, and fast. That is an almost perfect alarm system, and I would have thought useful also to badgers. But when we watched a group of badgers feeding together and one became alarmed for some reason, then we might see that one badger scamper off, leaving the others unaware of impending disaster. The badger's geographical range includes regions where wolves, lynxes, bears, and other enemies do or did occur, and in Britain man or dogs could be dangerous. An alarm system would have been useful, at least occasionally. Badgers did make one sound when confronted with sudden danger, a loud snort. It was not an alarm, in that from the context in which we observed it, it was clear that it was not meant to warn others, for instance a badger walking on its own and suddenly literally bumping into an observer. More likely, the biological function was to startle the would-be predator—and certainly I got quite a jolt on the various occasions when I was suddenly snorted at, at such close quarters.

The *snort* was a distinct, explosive sound, without any tonal quality. But the rest of the badger's vocabulary was more of a problem, a graded complex. One common call was the *gurgle*, to which we sometimes also referred as pant-grunt or staccato-grunt. These words themselves describe something of the quality of the sound, a soft, rumbling, rapid volley of very short grunts. I have heard this only produced by males, in two different kinds of contexts: when they were chasing or attacking an intruder, or when they followed a female during oestrus, and during mounting attempts. It indicated high excitement, as well as aggression and/or sexual attraction, and, as so often with calls, for its interpretation it had to be considered in context.

To demonstrate this last point: there was another sound which I named *soft-gurgle*, very similar to the previous one but quite a bit softer still. But this one was used only by the sow when she was with her cubs; most often, we heard it when she approached the entrance of a sett, sometimes carrying a piece of food. Then the cubs would emerge and take the food or sniff the mother: it was used to call the cubs out. So the calls themselves, the gurgle and the soft-gurgle, were hardly different, but the context and the function were quite dissimilar.

In aggressive situations, the noise which we heard most often was the *growl*, an apparently ubiquitous sound of carnivores and meaning more or less the same everywhere: defence. Male and female badgers used it, but there were different types of growls. When it was high pitched I called it a *wail*, but it was impossible to say where one became the other; in general, the higher the pitch, the more likely it was that the badger who produced it was being mauled. So low pitch meant more aggression, high pitch more fear. But sometimes also growls and gurgles were difficult to distinguish, again grading into each other.

To add a further label to this recital, whenever there was trouble in the clan, or when cubs were playing hard, we heard a sound which we named *keckering*, an onomatopoeia which probably describes some of the quality. It was a high-pitched gurgle, from either sex or badger of any age, defensive, and often associated with biting back more than with initiating aggression.

These somewhat clinical descriptions do not convey anything like the confusion met in the field, when these noises issued from a ball of playing, fighting, or mating badgers, and each call with every possible variation. Perhaps it is possible to make some generalizations about sounds: pitch indicates aggression or fear (the lower end of the scale being aggression, the higher end fear), whilst the staccato or rattling quality, the fast repetition in a series of sounds, increases with the general level of excitement, or conflict of motivations of the animal. A very similar set of general rules underlies the system of sound communication in the spotted hyaena which is a highly vocal species with a very diverse 'language'. There would therefore appear to be much scope for vocal expression by badgers, but their use of this kind of communication appears to be minimal.

Compared with other carnivores, especially with the social ones, badgers are very inarticulate animals. Whatever sign language they have available, they use very little; perhaps they have the means to make up for this with olfactory methods. To me, this question was important, because I tried to understand the reasons for badgers' sociality, but without knowing the mechanisms involved the question of function can never be solved properly. Although these purely behavioural problems appear to deviate from the main ecological concerns, I hope to show later that they are relevant.

ASPECTS OF SCENT COMMUNICATION

'To smell like a badger' is never meant as a compliment, which is somewhat strange because a badger does not really smell that offensively. But its body odour is very characteristic and easily remembered; it is a not very strong, somewhat soapy, rancid smell. A badger smells like that all over, but strongest in the tail region. I do not know whether the all-over effect is due to skin secretions on all parts of the body, or whether it originates from just the anal region. Badgers have several behaviour patterns which could ensure that all members of the clan are covered all over by the scent of the others. I will describe these below.

There are scent glands in many parts of the skin and on the feet, but there is no doubt that most of the secretions are produced in the anal region. This is obvious from the behaviour of the animals and from the discoloration of the hair around the tail caused by the secretions (Plate 21), immediately visible when the animals are walking around. Badgers scent-mark frequently; when a badger forages somewhere in the territory, it soon begins to carry out quick, squatting movements, often on no particular object, but perhaps on a clump of grass or a stone. We called it *squat-marking* (Plate 23).

During squat-marking the whole anal region touched whatever was being pressed, and as a result it was not just the product of one gland that was deposited, but a cocktail of various secretions. This was most obvious when a badger squat-marked in the snow (Plate 22). When we found the typical tracks of a scent-marking badger we could collect the faintly discoloured snow from the relevant spot for analysis in the laboratory. We found a mixture of secretions from the anal glands and the sub-caudal gland, as well as faecal matter. There was the potential for a long message in that, for a whole olfactorial sentence.

Two, large, anal glands are situated just inside the anus and open into the intestine; the pouches of these glands are under muscular control, so a badger can discharge whenever the scent is needed, in whatever quantity. Some of the anal gland secretions are also highly volatile and therefore useful at short range and for immediate, behavioural interactions. On badger latrines a kind of jelly can often be found, deposited with the faeces, or sometimes instead of faeces in the small dung-pits. I used to think that it was the product of the anal glands, and many people still think so, but I was mistaken. In the laboratory we found that the anal gland secretion is something quite different, and the jelly must originate somewhere much further down in the intestine. Almost certainly that jelly, too, carries some kind of signal, but the message remains mysterious.

I will have to leave the subject of anal glands as a set of open questions, but we have been able to find out something about that very important other gland, the huge one that is specific to the European badger and, to my knowledge, is not found in any other species—the sub-caudal gland. As the name indicates, it is situated immediately under the tail and above the anus (Plate 21); in fact, it could easily be mistaken for the anus itself at first glance. It is a very large pocket, several centimetres deep and wide (Fig. 9.4), and filled with a thick, white, creamy paste, sometimes as much as five or six cubic centimetres, or several teaspoonfuls. I wondered what was the function of that enormous and very unusual gland: did it have anything to do with the badgers' social life and organization?

I was fortunate that in the Zoology Department of Aberdeen University,

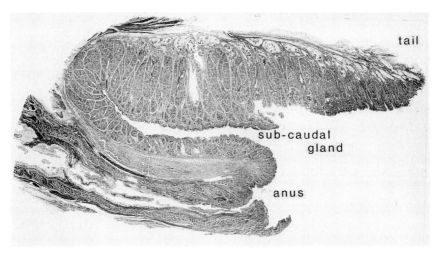

FIG. 9.4. Section through the sub-caudal gland of an adult male badger. The gland is a large pouch surrounded by sebaceous glands (From Gorman *et al.* 1984).

close to our Institute, Martyn Gorman was equally fascinated by the smell of the badger; animal smells are his speciality. So we decided on a joint project on the badgers' sub-caudal gland: what are the secretions, when are they produced, which badgers produce them and which animals respond, what messages can be carried? We realized that it was only one of the many aspects of scent communication in the badger, but it was obviously very significant; the gland was easily accessible and secretions could be taken out without difficulty. At least this sub-caudal gland might provide us with a small view into the world of badger scents and it might shed light on the problem of badger sociality.

To start with we analysed the secretion, the paste from the sub-caudal gland, to see what elements it consisted of and how those elements varied. Martyn did this in the laboratory in the university using gas–liquid chromatography. I will not go into details of the method, but essentially it produced a 'chromatograph' on which the main constituents of the paste were charted in the shape of peaks (Fig. 9.5). We did not know which chemical compounds these peaks represented, but we could number the peaks, measure their size, and compare their occurrence in different secretions; for our purpose, that was exactly what was needed. The convenience of a chromatograph was that we could look at it; it translated an olfactory pattern into a visual one. There were snags to this method of

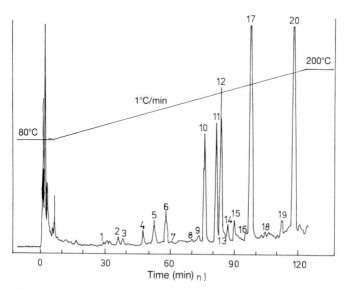

Fig. 9.5. A typical gas–liquid chromatograph of sub-caudal gland secretion. The temperature programme used in the analysis is shown on the figure. The numbered peaks are those used in the statistical analyses (from Gorman et al. 1984).

studying scents, which we had to ignore. The main problem was that what the chromatograph showed was not necessarily the same as what a badger smelt (that depended on the sensitivity of its nose to the different components).

From every badger we caught we collected the sub-caudal gland secretion, literally spooning it out, and of course we used our captive badgers, whom we could catch every few weeks and sample. We were also given a large collection of secretions from badgers which had been killed in the south of England in the TB eradication campaign by the Ministry of Agriculture. These samples were particularly valuable, because there were so many of them and because they came from badgers of known clan origin. These samples came from Chris Cheeseman's study area in the Cotswolds. Once we had a good collection of 'scent profiles', we compared them, with exciting results.

We looked at the 20 most striking peaks in the scent profiles. First, there were large differences between individual animals, in the relative size of the peaks, so at least gas–liquid chromatography could detect differences between them. Second, males and females were just as different from each other as they were between themselves for all the peaks that we looked at; in other words, there was no overall sex difference. But there were overall differences between the clans. For instance, in the samples from the Cotswolds the smell of a badger from what was known as the Gullet clan was much more like the smell of a clan mate than that of the neighbouring Convent clan badgers, and a Lake clan member was different again, but much more similar to other Lake clan badgers. We had the secretions of 39 badgers from 9 different clans, and each clan had its own scent profile, its own smell, with individual variations between badgers within the clan.

Thus a relatively simple chemical analysis showed that the badgers had the potential to use a system of individual and clan smells. Further questions then arose. Were such clan smells inherited or transferred between members? What would happen when badgers changed clans? It soon appeared that these questions were too simple. First of all, we noticed that the smells did not just vary between badgers, but that in each individual badger the composition of the secretion altered with time. But the change in a badger's smell was slow. When we compared the smell of a badger with its own smell of two or three months previously, then these two were statistically more similar than the odours of any two different badgers, but only just. In other words, if we wanted to recognize a badger from other badgers by the smell of its sub-caudal gland, we had to meet it again within about three months. This would also be true if a badger wanted to recognize another badger, but only if its nose was as good as or better than our gas chromatograph.

These analyses gave us at least some idea of the potential information that can be transmitted by the secretion of that one gland. We also realized that that information was probably not meant for fast, behavioural exchanges; none of the components were very volatile. But from the complexity of these scent profiles we might conclude that there could be as much information in the white paste as we could get from a picture of someone's face.

To obtain evidence about the way in which badgers used the information from the sub-caudal gland, we did a series of experiments with our captive animals. The following is an account of some of those trials.

An evening at the badger pen at our Institute, surrounded by trees, and sounds of cattle in the distance. August 1977, 20.00 hours. Rumpy, a large, very co-operative old boar, is at the wire netting, looking at Alan Leitch, who is helping us with the experiments. Alan sits, quietly, poking a small stick through the netting, a stick with a small quantity of white paste at the end. Rumpy sniffs it for a second or two, then looks up at Alan. The stick is withdrawn, and another one poked through. Rumpy sniffs again, and this time walks quickly to a small tray, hanging from the fence a short distance away. In it, he finds a peanut, just one; the reward. He snaps it up, and returns again to his place, waiting for the next stick. The badger is a very patient one; he goes through scores of trials like this. And he learns: after the smell of one particular badger he will get his award, and after another smell there will not be anything in the tray. Alan has contrived a way of getting a peanut in the tray without the badger noticing it; the only clue that Rumpy has is the smell on the stick. Tonight it takes about forty trials before the badger picks up the difference, and he has been confronted with this particular combination of secretions on three previous evenings already. But then, tonight, there is no mistaking.

We realized that we had to be very careful with this kind of experiment; we have to make absolutely certain that the badger does not get any clues from Alan, however slight. So after Rumpy appears to have learned the different smells, every so often during the following trials I give Alan some numbered sticks with scents, of which Alan also does not know from which badger they come, and with those there will be no peanut, whatever the badger does. If Rumpy still does the right thing with these 'blind' trials, if he still goes to the tray when the scent comes from the right badger, then he has scored a plus, he had a correct choice. Hours after we started, Rumpy responds correctly to more than 90 per cent of the presentations.

With these experiments we were studying what the badgers could possibly smell in the sub-caudal gland secretions, not just what a sophisticated laboratory instrument could do. And there was no doubt: badgers could distinguish between smells from various clan mates and strangers; they could pick out the smell of several 'friends' from those of several different 'foes'. So we knew then what the potential use was for this odour, in our highly artificial experiments; we now wanted to know what the badgers actually did with that capability.

The chemical profiles of the scent had shown us that no category of badger was particularly outstanding; all profiles were different, but there was nothing that distinguished males from females, or a dominant animal from the rest. However, as far as sheer quantities were concerned, the picture was quite different. The sub-caudal gland was about 2.5 times larger in males than in females, and at any one time a male had four times as much of the secretion in the pouch of the gland. A sow with cubs had more of the paste than sows without cubs. These differences also showed in the behaviour of badgers, at least in our captive animals: a dominant boar squat-marked 2.5 times per minute, a sow with cubs 0.7 times, and sows without cubs 0.3 times, all significantly different rates.

Squat-marking was done in three different situations. First, we saw it anywhere in the territory on the ground, on hummocks, or on logs (Plate 23); most often it occurred on the boundaries (near the latrines) and near the sett. Second, badgers did it on each other (Fig. 9.6): within the clan all badgers do it on all others, but most often the dominant male on the females and the mother sow on her cubs—in fact, the cubs were the category that was squat-marked more than any other. Third, badgers squat-marked the

FIG. 9.6. Adult boar badger (left) squat-marking on another member of the clan. Cub in foreground, another male behind, right. (Photograph by R. Tanner.)

bundles of bedding which they dragged into their sett. I will describe these scent-marking occasions in more detail.

The territorial boundaries were distinguished by many latrines which served as the boundary markers (Chapter 6). In Wytham I had found that 70 per cent of badger latrines were near territorial borders; with their scrapes, droppings, anal gland secretions, jellies, and squat-mark stations they had to be mines of information to a passing badger. Squat-marking was clearly concentrated near those places. Interestingly, when I took my tame badger, Tim, for walks on a lead, he always squat-marked several times near the places where he defecated, quite far from his artificial 'sett'. But that behaviour was also common close to the sett itself, where there were usually one or more latrines as well. So both the periphery and the hub of the territory was pasted by the owners.

We could conclude from our observations on the badgers themselves that in the territory all the clan members had the same odour as was distributed throughout the range, the same clan scent. This was brought about not only by individual secretions being rather similar, but also by animals frequently squat-marking each other. A male walked up to a female near the sett, she cowered, growled, then he turned round and squat-marked her rump, and she immediately stopped growling. It seemed to act as an appeasement, as an extra incentive for the male to squat-mark her; we have seen it on numerous occasions (in 44 per cent of 81 observations a sow was less aggressive to the boar after he marked her, only once was she more so, and in the other observations we saw no difference). In addition we saw not only male squatting on female, but it happened more or less frequently between all members of the clan, usually on each other's rump, which, incidentally, was also the part of the body which was sniffed most often when badgers met (Fig. 9.7).

By far the most exciting social scenting event was the 'mutual squat-mark'. Exciting not only because the badgers themselves were often rather worked up, but also because of the way in which we could interpret their behaviour.

Watching near the main Loch sett in Speyside, May 1980, late in the evening. One of the clan boars comes rustling back to the entrances, and I can see that he carries a radio-transmitter. I switch on my receiver: it is a youngish animal, which has been away from the main sett for a couple of days, staying in an outlier, about a kilometre away. He scratches around a bit, then meets an old sow, which may well be his mother. A brief, almost cursory sniff along the flanks by both, then they both turn around, and they back up against each other, tails up, rubbing their anal regions together. Seconds later they both go their own way again, staying around the sett, but more or less ignoring each other.

We called it the *mutual squat-mark*, not seen very frequently (compared with

FIG. 9.7. Two badgers sniffing each other's rump when meeting at the sett. This is also the part of the body that is scent marked most often. (Photograph by R. Tanner.)

the normal squat-mark of one badger onto the rump or flank of another), but especially during meetings after a longish absence. When in our group of captives we isolated one for a few days, then released it again with its clan mates, immediately there would be a spate of mutual squat-marking.

We could possibly interpret this mutual squat-mark as an accidental variation of the ordinary squat, where the two participants just happened to be doing the same thing on each other at the same time. However, Martyn Gorman and I thought that there was more to it. It is known that many animal scents (especially from carnivores) are in fact produced by bacteria, and in anal and other glands whole bacterial floras are known to exist, feeding on the glandular products of their host and producing the smells which we think are so characteristic of the various species of carnivores. We speculated that this might also be happening in and around the sub-caudal gland of badgers; if that were so, the mutual squat-mark might be a mechanism whereby clan members 'infect' each other with their bacteria. In this manner, badgers from the same clan could achieve their clan smell. It would suggest that badgers have to keep in contact with the rest of the clan at fairly regular intervals, in order to maintain the right odour. The mutual squat-mark would also provide a mechanism for integration into the clan; once a complete outsider would manage to mix its sub-caudal bacterial flora with clan members, a new, common clan odour would be assured.

A similar purpose might well underly the scent marking of the badgers' bedding. The bracken, or straw, or whatever dry vegetation lined the chambers in a sett, had a strong sub-caudal smell and no doubt it would rub off on any animal which slept in it. This would suit clan members which need to maintain the right body odour; it could also explain why badgers, in a series of experiments we did with the captives, consistently refused to carry into the sett any bedding material which smelled of badgers other than clan members. All other bedding was often squat-marked, and immediately dragged inside.

A picture now emerged in which members of a badger clan maintain a clan odour by scent marking each other (especially on each others' rump and flank), for which there are immediate behavioural rewards in terms of appeasement, and they scent-mark their territory (especially in the boundary region and sett area). The theory behind this, advanced by Gosling (1982) for scent marking in mammals in general, is that an intruding badger will know what the clan odour is because it has probably met it on the border; if it now meets another badger, it will move down wind of it, or sniff its rump or flank (Fig. 9.7) to ascertain whether or not it belongs to that territory. If the other badger has the territorial smell, this means that it has an 'investment' in that territory: it may know all the feeding patches and/or have cubs there, and it will therefore be prepared to put up a good fight. In the jargon of sociobiology, the odour has established an 'asymmetry of contest'; it demonstrated before a fight started that one of the animals is going to put up an extremely determined defence.

Badgers seemed to have adapted this general principle for use in a society consisting of groups, of clans. The details of the sub-caudal recognition mechanism, with the huge gland quite unknown in other Mustelids, and the intricate patterns of social scent marking, could have evolved as an adaptation of communication behaviour to the group territorial system. If it has, it would be one of the few behavioural adaptations of the badger to its gregarious organization.

Further details

See Kruuk *et al.* (1984); Gorman *et al.* (1984). See also Ewer (1973); Gosling (1982); Macdonald (1980*a*, 1983); Maynard-Smith and Parker (1976); Pocock (1911); Roper *et al.* (1986); Stubbe (1971); Tinbergen (1959).

10

Some conclusions

IMPLICATIONS FOR MANAGEMENT AND CONSERVATION

I did not set out on this badger study with practical problems in mind; it was intended as an academic enquiry into social organization and its ecological background. However, in order to understand social systems, spatial organization, and evolution of the behaviour of a species it is necessary to ask questions which are very similar to those that have to be solved for successful management, so this kind of study is bound to have practical implications. Furthermore, like any other scientist I would be pleased if some of my results could be useful in a practical way, especially in conservation. It is difficult to avoid some proselytizing, so I will therefore point out a few aspects of this research which might be practically relevant.

Badgers, like almost all other carnivores, are often in conflict with people. First, they are popular with the general public: they look attractive, and even though most people never see them, they like to know that the badgers are there. But badgers have disappeared from some areas, especially on the Continent: conservation management is called for, and badgers are protected and even transplanted to recolonize lost ground. Conservationists also protect badgers against unscrupulous people who dig out the animals to use them in 'badger baiting', setting dogs on them for sport. On the other hand, because of its behaviour the species is frequently in direct conflict with man, especially by inflicting damage on agriculture.

The nuisance value of badgers may take several forms: they may harm crops (maize, wheat, oats, barley, grapes), they may occasionally take livestock (lambs and poultry), they may damage fences (letting in rabbits) or dig holes in fields large enough even for tractors to get stuck in, and shepherds may lose their terriers to badgers when digging for foxes. Gamekeepers complain about badgers raiding pheasant nests and gardeners may suffer when badgers dig up their lawns. But all this pales into insignificance compared with the harm badgers do by transmitting diseases, especially bovine tuberculosis (TB) to cattle in Britain and rabies in continental Europe. This transmission of disease is well documented and I will not discuss it further. It is in the context of these problems that some of the Scottish results could be useful.

Immediate, practical spin-offs are the methods we developed for measuring badgers' ranges and population sizes. Providing wild badgers with peanuts and colour markers, then mapping the distribution of these markers in territorial border latrines, is a quick and efficient method of assessing the animals' range size, and range size is one of the first aspects of their life we need to know if we want to 'manage' them, be it for control or for protection. The method is widely used now by conservationists who want to know which badgers will be affected by a new road, but also especially by officials of the Ministry of Agriculture, Fisheries and Food (MAFF) in England when investigating which badger clans are in contact with a herd of cattle in which TB has been diagnosed. The method of estimating carnivore numbers from their faeces, calculating the percentage of the population which is excreting an injected isotope, is useful also for many other species, apart from badgers. A disadvantage of the method is that the use of isotopes is subject to legal restrictions and the necessary precautions when working with these materials are cumbersome. But to date there are very few, if any, suitable alternatives.

Other, incidental, practical results of our study can be applied only within the confines of the laws relevant to interfering with badgers. In several countries, especially in the UK, these laws are quite strict and explicit, and their details must be regarded if faced with a practical badger problem. There is now an excellent guide to practical problems with badgers and the law (Harris *et al.* 1988). Some of the Scottish experience is relevant; this includes the usefulness of our large cage-traps for catching the animals, or the advice we can give to farmers or gardeners who want to keep badgers out of a particular outlier sett. Knowledge of the social system of the species, its use of main setts and outliers, indicates that it is quite often possible, without substantial detriment to a badger clan, to remove outlier setts (or make them uninhabitable) if they interfere with farming or with a road or whatever.

An important observation could be that generally low-ranking animals in the clan are more likely to spend the day in outlying setts than the dominant, resident boars and sows. Although I am now speculating, it may well be that diseased badgers, too, would be more inclined to use the small, inconspicuous outliers rather than the large, central main setts. If that is the case they would be less likely to be caught if a central sett is trapped out or gassed for disease control purposes, which is the present MAFF policy in areas where TB is suspected amongst badgers.

One aspect of our work which is highly relevant for conservationists involved with badgers is that relating to the animals' territoriality. In this book I have shown that the badgers' ferocious defence of their area against others of the same sex plays a very important role throughout their lives; the implication of this is that great care has to be taken when releasing strange badgers in unknown territory. Badgers, males as well as females, are ferocious fighters, and introductions of new animals in areas where there are badgers already present have little chance of success. It is also unlikely that new introductions may be able to find a niche somewhere in between existing clans; as new arrivals they would not get a chance. But also introductions in areas without badgers are often unlikely to succeed, mostly because the species is usually absent from such places for good reason. Transplantations should be undertaken only to areas which are suitable for the species, where there are no other badgers, and where the reason for the badgers' absence is fully understood but is no longer operating.

We ourselves have been able to move badgers into a new area: we simply opened the gates of our enclosure with captive badgers at the end of the study. There were no other badgers around, it was good badger habitat with wooded slopes and many small, grazed pastures, and the reason for the previous absence of the species was quite likely the heavy hand of local gamekeepers, snaring for foxes and other 'vermin'. Keepering is very much reduced now, and we thought that the badgers would stand a good chance. We followed the release of four of the badgers with radio-transmitters; it took them many days before they left the safety of their enclosure, but finally they settled nearby, digging themselves new setts, establishing latrine sites—but still often using the artificial setts in their enclosure, even now, three years later. There are now at least three (probably more) separate clans within a mile of our research station and the release appears to have been a success.

Although much of what I have said before about badger ecology revolved around food, it was clear also that a prerequisite for badger habitat is the presence of suitable sites for their setts. In the usual agricultural areas where badgers live in a large, central sett, where they use a central-place foraging strategy, the animals need to have well-drained soils for the sett, or small caves or groups of boulders, preferably on slopes and preferably wooded. I think it is this requirement which is behind the absence of the species from large tracts of agricultural land in the east of England and from the flatter areas on the Continent. Potential sett sites should be a major consideration in the assessment of the suitability of an area for badgers.

But if sites for setts are available, then most of the rest of badger ecology revolves around food, and this study has shown the overriding importance of earthworms in many regions of north-west Europe. One factor which influences the availability of earthworms on the surface is the length of the grass in pastures, and this is a major variable in the hands of management. We have shown that long grass makes it impossible for badgers to feed efficiently: they need short, grazed pasture. There are two important consequences of this observation. First, short-grass grazed pastures are the major contact points between cattle and badgers and probably play a vital role in the transmission of TB between the species. If this is indeed correct, then attempts to control this transmission could be directed at pasture management; perhaps it is not unrealistic to think in terms of reducing worm populations, or of cattle grazing regimes. And this becomes somewhat more realistic when we consider the second point I want to make. It is quite possible that badger populations in several parts of Europe are much lower than they could be (certainly much lower than in England), because of the practice of keeping cattle indoors, managing the grasslands not for grazing but for silage and hay. In Germany, for instance, very large tracts of tall grassland can be seen, many kilometres square, fields without fences, and often not a single cow. There are many potential sites for badger setts, but as far as food is concerned such areas are quite unsuitable for badgers and the species are rare or absent there.

Perhaps this, and the observations described in the previous chapters, puts our relationship with badgers into a somewhat different perspective. There is little doubt that in most parts of Europe, including Britain, badger populations, their density, the size of their clans, the area of their territory, their food selection and foraging strategies, are almost totally dependent on agriculture or other human activities. This means that as conservationists concerned with the survival of badgers, or as farmers concerned about this species' impact on livestock, we are trying to protect or manage not an aspect of untouched wilderness, but one of the corollaries of traditional agriculture. Many aspects of badger populations are of our own making and they have evolved over many years of land management, of badgers being commensal to our agricultural activities. This should in no way detract from the enjoyment we can get from the animals, but at the same time we should not be afraid to interfere with their relationship with us and cultivate it or restrain it, just as we would manage traditional hedgerows, for instance.

One of the messages from the Scottish studies is that in designing management policies for badgers, for whatever purpose, the peculiar social structure of badger populations has to be considered: the existence of groups which are almost independent sub-populations, in their own group territories, clans in which numbers and area sizes are related to different aspects of food biomass and distribution. Overall population density is for many purposes less meaningful than group size and range size, earthworm biomass is in some aspects less important to badgers than earthworm dispersion. An understanding of these relationships in any one area enables us to define the needs of badger populations, of clans of badgers: such understanding should be the first step in management.

WHY CLANS?

In the Scottish Highlands I have been studying not 'The Badger', but merely a few of the many manifestations of its ecological and behavioural organization. I have been looking at the same species which lives more or less solitarily in central and southern Europe, or densely packed in group territorial compartments in the south of England, or in apparent suburban disarray in large cities.

This realization puts much of what I have seen in an interesting perspective; it means that badgers do not *have* to be like this. Their organization is not something left over from the days when their social system evolved. It means that the behaviour and social system I watched is likely to be adapted to the environment here and now, and what I saw is probably the most efficient way for the badgers to behave and to be organized, within the limits of the species' potential. It validates the basis for my questioning: how is this animal adjusted to its environment?

My main question at the outset of this badger project was the one that appeared to be central to the social organization of this species: why should badgers live in groups? So far I have not answered that question here, mainly because it was too simplistic. One of the lessons Niko Tinbergen taught us, in his brilliant book *The Study of Instinct*, was that in biology the question *Why?* had four different meanings. When I ask it in the context of the badgers' social organization it can be an enquiry into

(1) the causal mechanism (how does it work?);

(2) the ontogeny (how does it come about in the animals' lifetime?);

(3) the biological function (what is its adaptive value in the badgers' environment?); and

(4) its history (how has it evolved?).

I will summarize some of our main findings under these four headings.

The mechanism of group organization

In our study areas badgers are highly dependent on earthworms for food, and many aspects of their feeding, the seasonality in activity, and the badgers' foraging strategies are directed towards catching earthworms. Earthworms have a very clumped distribution, with concentrations in pastures and certain kinds of woodland. These concentrations of food are not all available at the same time, but depend on grass length (i.e. grazing by livestock), weather and micro-climate, and other factors. To have at least one productive patch available at any one time (or most of the time), a badger will need to have several worm concentrations in its home range; these worm concentrations or 'patches' should have worms on the surface at different times or under different conditions.

To maintain access to several earthworm patches badgers have the option of single-animal or single-pair territories with enough food for year-round survival and for reproduction. If these territories were to be as small as possible, this would imply that they would have very convoluted boundaries (Fig. 10.1), which would be difficult to defend. Territorial defence is extremely important to badgers; they are ferocious fighters and spend a great deal of time on defence and scent marking, which, again, is understandable. If a badger should lose only a small part of its area, it might lose a vital patch of food which would make the whole home range non-viable. Territorial defence is much more efficient if several home ranges are joined into an area with a small perimeter. Of course, this argument would apply to all neighbouring territories of all animals, but in most other territorial species the joining of territories would result in greatly enlarged areas and smaller benefits in terms of boundary to surface ratio than in the case of the badgers, with their 'temporal patches' of food.

There appears to be a strong advantage in keeping a territory small, and that may be the reason why badgers do not live in much larger areas in much larger groups. The advantage may be twofold. First, in terms of energy expenditure and proximity of a safe haven, the distance between sett and feeding areas should be minimized. Second, and more intangible, it is

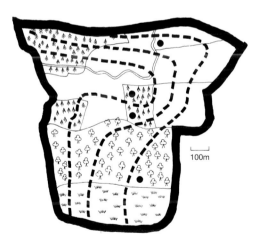

FIG. 10.1. Simplified map of the territory of the Sheilich clan, Speyside, with four adult badgers, different vegetation types, and the location of four setts (black dots). Superimposed are hypothetical boundaries which individual badgers would have to respect if they divided the territory between them, each having access to all major vegetation types (from Kruuk and Macdonald 1985).

probably necessary for a badger to know an area very well in order to exploit it efficiently. I frequently noticed badgers going directly from the sett to areas where there was a lot of food available on that particular night. They clearly know their range extremely well, and it seems likely that such detailed knowledge is more difficult to acquire or maintain for larger areas.

Basically, then, the mechanism of the group organization appears to be that a badger uses a specific area, the size of which is determined by food dispersion, and it does not put pressure on its offspring to leave until there is a shortage of resources, nor does its offspring emigrate soon after weaning. The number of badgers which can use a regularly shaped area with a patchy food supply, i.e. the group or clan size, depends on the food available during the leanest periods, which may be considerable because of the richness of the patches.

There are some possible alternative mechanisms for attaining a large group size, but none of these seems to be a suitable explanation in the case of the badger. For instance, individuals of a species might find it more efficient to co-operate in some activity, e.g. in hunting, or in digging holes, or defending against predators, or whatever. They might then live in groups and expand their territory accordingly. However, in badgers we found no evidence for co-operation between individuals in anything except in digging setts and sleeping in a huddle, and that only under certain conditions. Also, if a species lived in groups and adapted its territory according to the size of the group, the size of the territory and the size of group living in it might be expected to be correlated. In badgers that is not the case, but it does happen in coyotes, for instance, and in wolves. These species could be termed 'expansionists', whilst badgers would be 'contractors', keeping their territory as small as possible.

One difficulty with the hypothesis that relates territory and group size to the patchy distribution of food lies in the definition of a patch, of a clump of food. In the case of badgers, it is often easy to recognize well-delineated fields or copses with a high food biomass, and an agricultural landscape is almost proverbially patchy. But in many situations the food distribution is more blurred and both the size and the temporal availability of food patches can only be described in a highly arbitrary manner. This becomes even more of a problem in areas where badgers regularly take different kinds of food, instead of specializing in just one prey species, such as earthworms. In such cases a much more sophisticated analysis will need to be carried out than I have been able to do here, to understand the mechanism of larger group sizes.

The development of clans

We found that the number of cubs born into a clan was more or less constant over a large range of clan sizes; in other words, it is unlikely that this recruitment determines the size of the clan. Since immigration is rare and diffficult because of the high level of aggression towards strangers, the alternative, therefore, is that mortality and/or emigration limits the number of individual badgers per clan. It seems likely that, generally, a pair of badgers holds a territory, reproducing regularly, and that the clan size is determined by the age at which offspring leave the territory or die.

A resident territorial boar allows his sons to stay for many years, but he will be more aggressive towards them if food shortages arise. The younger boars will not, or not often, be able to mate within the clan, perhaps more because of the preference of the females ('incest-taboo') than because of competition with their father. To reproduce, they will have to either emigrate or sneak across the border and raid the neighbouring clan. In the Scottish study areas, males emigrated after several years, and always to a neighbouring clan; it appeared that they moved into a 'vacancy' of resident territorial male. Their strategy therefore seemed to be: if possible stay at home until a vacancy arises nearby, then take over another clan.

An alternative strategy for offspring would have been to start roaming around, looking for vacancies everywhere (this is what foxes do, for instance). It seems likely that this would have been less successful because of the highly aggressive territorial defence of the badger, in areas saturated with badger territories, and the chance of immediately finding a vacancy is very small. In other areas with a higher density of badgers (e.g. the Cotswolds in England), badger males appear to stay in their own clan range for their whole life, emigration being very rare, and it is likely that for many males their entire reproductive output is achieved by matings across territorial boundaries.

However, there must also be a number of males which do not obtain a territory and are just pushed out of the range, being forced to emigrate perhaps through aggression from the dominant resident boar. Those males end up either in a 'bachelor clan', as I found in Wytham, or in a solitary range squeezed in between clan ranges (or across their borders), as Paul Latour found in Speyside, or they roam about and disappear, perhaps settling somewhere in marginal habitat or in a clan far away. We noticed some of those 'disappearances', but we were never able to document exactly what happened to them.

Young females stay at home, sometimes expanding their range into that of the neighbouring clan, but we have no evidence of real emigration: they continue to use their natal clan range. Some females disappeared and perhaps settled in some unoccupied areas elsewhere, but the individual strategy appears to be to stay at home, even if this means no reproduction for many years or ever. The old, resident territorial sow allows her daughters in the territory, although the evidence is that she gets more aggressive when resources dwindle. But at least in captivity she becomes highly intolerant of her eldest daughter (the most likely other female to reproduce) at the time of parturition. It seems that for the younger females the advantages of exploiting the safe natal territory outweigh the disadvantage of only having a small chance of becoming the resident, breeding matriarch.

The adaptive value of living in a clan

It would almost appear as if badgers live in groups, in clans, by default: the clumped distribution of resources allows them to stay at home instead of facing the harsh realities beyond the borders. To that extent, the clan organization is an adaptation made feasible by the characteristics of their prey species, largely determined by our agricultural practice. But the adaptive value, the advantage of living in a clan, has clearly not been fully realized by the species, perhaps because evolution has not been able to move fast enough to make use of the opportunities afforded by our agricultural development. There is no hint of joint foraging, although we showed in captivity that badgers have the ability to co-operate in finding food. There is no joint defence against predators and badgers do not have an effective alarm call, so they do not even warn clan members of approaching danger, let alone defend each other against a predator (as for instances mongooses do). They do sleep in a huddle, and that must reduce heat loss and therefore have energy-saving advantages. Most, or all, clan members contribute to territorial defence, and that is likely to be advantageous to the whole group, but they do not do so jointly: there are no border patrol groups, as in spotted hyaenas, and in any case most of this defence is carried out by the oldest, dominant animals. There is no helping each other in the rearing of the cubs: males are not involved, neither are older siblings or other female relatives of the resident sow.

Perhaps the most telling 'deficiency' in adaptation is the lack of diversification in social behaviour, especially in communication; badgers are as inarticulate as any solitary Mustelid. There is a dearth of visual displays, of calls, and the only field in which, perhaps, badgers excel is in the use of scent. But smells are a primitive means of communication, with severe limitations in speed, directionality (depending on wind), and distance. Nevertheless, the badgers' use of the sub-caudal gland suggests that this behaviour could have evolved as an adaptation to life in a group.

Evolution of the clan

For the order Carnivora the evolutionary history is better known than for many other groups; there is much fossil evidence. It is generally agreed that the seven different families have evolved from a primitive, now extinct family Miacidae and the Mustelids, to which the badgers belong, have been a distinct family ever since they branched off from the Miacidae. They are, therefore, an old and rather primitive group, as are the Viverrids (genet cats and mongooses). This is in contrast with carnivore families such as the bears, the cats, and the hyaenas, which evolved later.

When we speculate on what the original, primitive behaviour of carnivores was from what we now know of them, certain assumptions have to be made. One of these assumptions is that the most common features of a group of animals are also the most primitive ones. For instance, in the case of social organization of carnivores we find as the 'normal' system single territorial females, with single males in independent and larger territories, completely overlapping those of the females. Females defend their area against other females, males defend a larger one against other males. It is likely that this system was also the social organization of the Miacidae, because it is found right through all the families of the carnivores, with the exception of the Canids (which basically live in pairs). The Mustelids fall into that pattern, too; but badgers are the clear exception to the rule that Mustelids are solitary animals, so we assume that the primitive condition was the single-animal single-sex territory, from which the clan system evolved.

This evolution of the clan system involved several steps, not necessarily in the order in which I mention them here. The animals came to tolerate relatives of the same sex in their territory, the territory of males became the same size as that of the female, the territorial boundaries of males and females became identical, and clan members lived together in the same den, the sett. Each of these changes could have been a consequence of the adaptive advantages derived from exploiting the temporal food patches, as discussed above, with one exception. That is the phenomenon of identical male–female territories; it is not immediately clear why most males should have evolved to content themselves with only one female territory. But perhaps this, too, comes back to the overriding need to keep the foraging territory as small as possible, without that need being outweighed even by the advantages of having several females breeding.

It is interesting that the phenomenon of a clan system, of group territories and gregarious living appears to have evolved independently in six of the seven carnivore familes (not in the bears). For instance, spotted hyaenas are the only gregarious species in the hyaena family; they hunt large ungulates, such as wildebeest, zebra, and gazelles, by running them down over distances of several kilometres. The other Hyaenids eat small vertebrates or insects, or they scavenge. In order to have enough space to hunt and pull down prey without straying into neighbouring territories, spotted hyaenas need a large area, which carries so many wildebeest and other ungulates that many more than one hyaena can be sustained. Consequently, hyaenas in the areas where I studied them lived in clans of up to 80 individuals, and within these clans they can behave in a solitary manner, or they can co-operate in hunting (in packs of up to 20 or more). They have communal dens, they go in packs on boundary patrols, and they have evolved a highly elaborate vocabulary of calls, as well as many displays, and they use various scents for olfactory communication, including marking purposes. In contrast, other Hyaenid species are much more inarticulate. In this case I think it is likely that the dispersion characteristics of food availability (the predator needs a large area, but within that there is a high prey biomass) are the bases of the gregarious social system, and developing from that the species evolved the various co-operative behaviour patterns and elaborate communication.

In the cat family the lion evolved in its organization of prides, and in the Viverrids we find packs with large group sizes in the banded mongoose, the dwarf mongoose, and in the suricates, with an evolution of social behaviour patterns similar to what we see in the spotted hyaena. In the Procyonid family it is the coati, and amongst the Canids the wolves and coyotes, which show gregarious systems; all these species have highly complicated communication behaviour patterns and various forms of co-operation. But in the Canid family there is also an apparent contradiction in another species, perhaps the one that confirms the rule—the African hunting dog. The hunting dog is an extremely gregarious and highly co-operative species; members of a pack rarely stray out of each others' sight, and its social system shows none of the frequent transitions between solitary and group life that occur in wolves, hyaenas, and lions. Hunting dogs, therefore, are so gregarious that there may not be a great advantage in having an elaborate communication system, and it is a very silent, undemonstrative species compared with wolves, coyotes, or foxes. There is extremely close co-operation between pack members in hunting, cub rearing, and in territory and anti-predator defence.

Compared with all these other carnivore species, the spotted hyaena, lion, wolf, suricate, and others, the badger's social system is primitive, rather undifferentiated, and only a small step removed from that of its solitary relatives in the Mustelid family. In fact, under different ecological conditions badgers can also revert to a more or less solitary existence. It is tempting to suggest that in the European badger we see the first step in the evolution of a gregarious society; the ecological basis is there, but the species has not yet evolved to realize the full potential of life in a clan. Perhaps given time and many generations of badgers in our present system of agriculture, they will yet become a fully adapted social species.

Further details

See Kruuk (1978a, 1972, 1975, 1986, 1987); Kruuk *et al.* (1979, 1980, 1986); Kruuk and Macdonald (1985); Kruuk and Mills (1983). See also Carr and Macdonald (1986); Cheeseman *et al.* (1981); Harris *et al.* (1988); Macdonald (1983); Neal (1986); Tinbergen (1951).

REFERENCES

Ahnlund, H. (1980). Seasonal maturity and breeding season of the badger in Sweden. *Journal of Zoology, London*, **190**, 77–95.

Ahnlund, H. (1981). Productivity and mortality of the badger, *Meles meles* L., in central Sweden. PhD Thesis, University of Stockholm.

Amlaner, C. J. and Macdonald, D. W. (eds) (1980). A handbook on biotelemetry and radiotracking. Pergamon Press, Oxford.

Andersen, J. (1955). The food of the Danish badger (*Meles meles danicus*). *Danish Review of Game Biology*, **3**, 1–75.

Anderson, R. M. and Trewhella, W. (1985). Population dynamics of the badger (*Meles meles*) and the epidemiology of bovine tuberculosis (*Mycobacterium bovis*). *Philosophical Transactions of the Royal Society of London*, B, **310**, 327–81.

Brown, C. A. J. (1983). Prey abundance of the European badger, *Meles meles*, in north-east Scotland. *Mammalia*, **47**, 81–6.

Carr, G. M. and Macdonald, D. W. (1986). The sociality of solitary foragers: a model based on resource dispersion. *Animal Behaviour*, **34**, 1540–9.

Cheeseman, C. L., and Mallinson, P. J. (1980). Radio tracking in the study of bovine tuberculosis in badgers. In *A handbook on biotelemetry and radiotracking*, (ed. C. J. Amlaner and D. W. Macdonald), pp. 649–56, Pergamon Press, Oxford.

Cheeseman, C. L., Little, T. W. A., Gallagher, J., and Mallinson, P. J. (1981). The population structure, density and prevalence of tuberculosis (*Mycobacterium bovis*) in badgers (*Meles meles*) from four areas in south-west England. *Journal of Applied Ecology*, **18**, 795–804.

Cheeseman, C. L., Wilesmith, J. W., Ryan, J., and Mallinson, P. J. (1987). Badger population dynamics in a high density area. *Symposium of the Zoological Society of London*, **58**, 279–94.

Cheeseman, C. L., Cresswell, W. J., Harris, S., and Mallinson, P. J. (1988). Comparison of dispersal and other movements in two badger (*Meles meles*) populations. *Mammal Review*, **18**, 51–9

Ciampalini, B. and Lovari, S. (1985). Food habits and niche overlap of the badger (*Meles meles* L.) and the red fox (*Vulpes vulpes* L.) in a Mediterranean coastal area. *Zeitschrift für Säugetierkunde*, **50**, 226–34.

Edwards, C. A. and Lofty, J. R. (1977). *Biology of earthworms*. Chapman and Hall, London.

Elton, C. S. (1966). *The pattern of animal communities*. Methuen, London.

Ewer, R. F. (1973) *The carnivores*. Weidenfeld & Nicolson, London.

Fowler, P. A. and Racey, P. A. (1988). Overwintering strategies of the badger, *Meles meles*, at 57°N. *Journal of Zoology, London*, **214**, 635–51.

Gorman, M. L., Kruuk, H., and Leitch, A. (1984). Social functions of the sub-caudal scent gland secretion of the European badger *Meles meles* (Carnivora: Mustelidae). *Journal of Zoology, London*, **204**, 549–59.

Gosling, L. M. (1982). A reassessment of the function of scent marking in territories. *Zeitschrift für Tierpsychologie*, **60,** 89–118.

Harris, S. (1982). Activity patterns and habitat utilization of badgers (*Meles meles*) in suburban Bristol: a radio tracking study. *Symposia of the Zoological Society of London*, **58,** 295–311.

Harris, S. and Cresswell, W. J. (1987). Dynamics of a suburban badger (*Meles meles*) population. *Symposia of the Zoological Society of London*, **58,** 295–311.

Harris, S., Jefferies, D., and Cresswell, W. (1988). *Problems with badgers?* RSPCA Publications, Horsham.

Kollmannsperger, F. (1955). Über Rhythmen bei Lumbriciden. *Decheniana*, **108,** 81–92.

Kruuk, H. (1972). *The spotted hyena.* University of Chicago Press, Chicago.

Kruuk, H. (1975). Functional aspects of social hunting by carnivores. In *Function and evolution in behaviour*, (ed. G. Baerends, C. Beer, and A. Manning), pp. 119–41, Clarendon Press, Oxford.

Kruuk, H. (1978a). Spatial organisation and territorial behaviour of the European badger *Meles meles*. *Journal of Zoology (London)*, **184,** 1–19.

Kruuk, H. (1978b). Foraging and spatial organisation of the European badger, *Meles meles* L. *Behavioural Ecology and Sociobiology*, **4,** 75–89.

Kruuk, H. (1986). Dispersion of badgers *Meles meles* (L., 1758) and their resources: a summary. *Lutra*, **29,** 12–15.

Kruuk, H. (1987). The case of the clannish badger. *Natural History, New York*, **95(12),** 50–7.

Kruuk, H. and de Kock, L. (1981). Food and habitat of badgers (*Meles meles*) on Monte Baldo, northern Italy. *Zeitschrift für Säugetierkunde*, **48,** 45–50.

Kruuk, H. and Macdonald, D. (1985). Group territories of carnivores: empires and enclaves. In *Behavioural ecology: ecological consequences of adaptive behaviour*, (ed. R. M. Sibly and R. H. Smith), pp. 521–36, Blackwell Scientific, Oxford.

Kruuk, H. and Mills, M. G. L. (1983). Notes on food and foraging of the honey badger *Mellivora capensis* in the Kalahari Gemsbok National Park. *Koedoe*, **26,** 153–7.

Kruuk, H. and Parish, T. (1977). *Behaviour of badgers.* Institute of Terrestrial Ecology, Cambridge.

Kruuk, H. and Parish T. (1981). Feeding specialization of the European badger *Meles meles* in Scotland. *Journal of Animal Ecology*, **50,** 773–88.

Kruuk, H. and Parish, T. (1982). Factors affecting population density, group size and territory size of the European badger *Meles meles*. *Journal of Zoology, London*, **196,** 31–9.

Kruuk, H. and Parish, T. (1983). Seasonal and local differences in the weight of European badgers (*Meles meles*) in relation to food supply. *Zeitschrift für Säugetierkunde*, **48,** 45–50.

Kruuk, H. and Parish, T. (1985). Food, food availability and weight of badgers (*Meles meles*) in relation to agricultural changes. *Journal of Applied Ecology*, **22,** 705–15.

Kruuk, H. and Parish, T. (1987). Changes in the size of groups and ranges of the

European badger (*Meles meles* L.) in an area in Scotland. *Journal of Animal Ecology*, **56**, 351–64.

Kruuk, H., Parish, T., Brown, C. A. J., and Carrera, J. (1979). The use of pasture by the European badger (*Meles meles*). *Journal of Applied Ecology*, **16**, 453–9.

Kruuk, H., Gorman, M., and Parish, T. (1980). The use of ^{65}Zn for estimating populations of carnivores. *Oikos*, **34**, 206–8.

Kruuk, H., Gorman, M. L., and Leitch, A. (1984). Scent marking with the subcaudal gland by the European badger *Meles meles* L. *Animal Behaviour*, **32**, 899–907.

Kruuk, H., Miller, S., and Pike, A. (1986). Badger release. *Scottish Wildlife*, **22**, 13–15.

Latour, P. B. (1988). The individual within the group territorial system of the European badger (*Meles meles* L.). PhD Thesis, University of Aberdeen.

Lawrence, R. D. and Millar, H. R. (1945). Protein content of earthworms. *Nature (London)*, **155**, 517.

Leitch, A. and Kruuk, H. (1986). Birds eaten by badgers *Meles meles* (L., 1758) in Scotland. *Lutra*, **29**, 16–20.

Macdonald, D. W. (1980*a*). Patterns of scent marking with urine and faeces among carnivore communities. *Symposia of the Zoological Society of London*, **45**, 107–39.

Macdonald, D. W. (1980*b*). The red fox, *Vulpes vulpes*, as a predator upon earthworms. *Zeitschrift für Tierpsychologie*, **52**, 171–200.

Macdonald, D. W. (1983). The ecology of carnivore social behaviour. *Nature (London)*, **301**, 379–84.

Macdonald, D. W. and Moehlman, P. D. (1983). Cooperation, altruism and restraint in the reproduction of carnivores. In *Perspectives in ethology*, vol. 5, (ed. P. P. G. Bateson and P. Klopfer), pp. 433–66, Plenum Press, New York.

Maynard-Smith, J. and Parker, G. A. (1976). The logic of asymmetric contests. *Animal Behaviour*, **24**, 159–75.

Mellgren, R. L. and Roper, T. J. (1986). Spatial learning and discrimination of food patches in the European badger (*Meles meles* L.). *Animal Behaviour*, **34**, 1129–34.

Mouches, A. (1981). Variations saisonnières du régime alimentaire chez le blaireau européen (*Meles meles*). *Revue Ecologie (Terre et Vie)*, **35**, 183–94.

Neal, E. (1948). *The badger*. Collins, London.

Neal, E. (1977). *Badgers*. Blandford Press, Poole.

Neal, E. (1986). *The natural history of badgers*. Christopher Helm, London.

Neal, E. and Harrison, R. J. (1958). Reproduction in the European badger (*Meles meles*). *Transactions of the Zoological Society of London*, **29**, 67–130.

Paget, R. J. and Middleton, A. L. V. (1974). *Badgers of Yorkshire and Humberside*. Ebor Press, York,

Parish, T. (1980). A collapsible dipole antenna for radio tracking on 102 MHz. In *A handbook of biotelemetry and radio tracking*, (ed. C. J. Amlaner and D. W. Macdonald), pp. 263–8, Pergamon Press, Oxford.

Parish, T. and Kruuk, H. (1983). The uses of radio tracking combined with other techniques in studies of badger ecology in Scotland. *Symposia of the Zoological Society of London*, **49**, 291–9.

Pigozzi, G. (1987). Behavioural ecology of the European badger (*Meles meles*): diet, food availability and use of space in the Maremma Natural Park, Central Italy. PhD Thesis, University of Aberdeen.

Pocock, I. (1911). Some probable and possible instances of warning characteristics amongst insectivorous and carnivorous mammals. *Annals and Magazine of Natural History*, **8**, 750–7.

Powell, R. A. (1979). Mustelid spacing patterns: variations on a theme by Mustela. *Zeitschrift für Tierpsychologie*, **50**, 153–65.

Roper, T. J., Sheperdson, D. J., and Davies, J. M. (1986). Scent marking with faeces and anal secretion in the European badger (*Meles meles*): seasonal and spatial characteristics of latrine use in relation to territoriality. *Behaviour*, **97**, 94–117.

Satchell, J. E. (1967). Lumbricidae. In *Soil biology*, (ed. A. Burgess and F. Raw), pp. 259–322, Academic Press, London.

Skoog, P. (1970). The food of the Swedish badger, *Meles meles* L. *Viltrevy*, **7**, 1–120.

Smith, J. N. M. (1974). The food searching behaviour of two European thrushes, I. Description and analysis of search paths. *Behaviour*, **48**, 276–302.

Stubbe, M. (1971). Die analen Markierungsorganen des Dachsen, *Meles meles* (L.). *Der Zoologische Garten N. F., Leipzig*, **40**, 125–35.

Tinbergen, N. (1951). *The study of instinct*. Clarendon Press, Oxford.

Tinbergen, N. (1959). Comparative studies of the behaviour of gulls (Laridae). *Behaviour*, **15**, 1–70.

INDEX